Trees, Shrubs,

and Vines

of the

Texas Hill Country

SECOND EDITION

Number Thirty-nine
Louise Lindsey Merrick Natural Environment Series

Trees, Shrubs, and Vines of the Texas Hill Country

A FIELD GUIDE

Second Edition

Jan Wrede

TEXAS A&M UNIVERSITY PRESS

COLLEGE STATION

The paper used in this book meets the minimum requirements
of the American National Standard for Permanence
of Paper for Printed Library Materials, Z39.48-1984.
Binding materials have been chosen for durability.
Manufactured in China through Martin Book Management.

Library of Congress Cataloging-in-Publication Data

Wrede, Jan, 1943–
    Trees, shrubs, and vines of the Texas Hill Country : a field guide /
Jan Wrede. — Rev. ed.
        p. cm. — (Louise Lindsey Merrick Natural Environment
Series; no. 39)
    Includes bibliographical references and index.
    ISBN-13: 978-1-60344-188-9 (flexbind : alk. paper)
    ISBN-10: 1-60344-188-3 (flexbind : alk. paper)
    1. Woody plants—Texas—Texas Hill Country—Identification.
I. Title.   II. Series: Louise Lindsey Merrick Natural Environment Series; no. 39.
QK188.W74   2010
582.16'09764—dc22
2009030510

This book is dedicated to you,

the reader, who will use it to

understand, appreciate, and preserve

one of the Texas Hill Country's

best-kept secrets: its native trees,

shrubs, and vines.

Contents

Acknowledgments

Creation of this book was a labor of love from beginning to end. Seven years ago, Mark Peterson, who had faith in my ability, and Kim Kuebel, who became my personal plant guru, gave me the courage to write and publish the first edition of this book, *Texans Love Their Land.*

Many others gave essential helping hands along the way. Family, friends, and acquaintances listened to me talk endlessly about woody plants and land stewardship, made comments, and gave advice. Bill Ward taught me Texas Hill Country geology. Rufus Stephens, Mark Peterson, Paula Witt, Chris and Dick Park, and my sister Peggy Sankey read parts of the manuscript and made substantial contributions. Rebecca Yoder and Linda McMahan lent essential assistance with the resources section. Anne Adams, Eric Beckers, Kim Kuebel, John Millsaps, Emily Rogers, Susan Sander, Bill Ward, Steve Nelle, Michael Margo, and Rufus Stephens contributed photographs. Steve Nelle, Jackie Poole, Bill Carr, Patty Leslie-Pasztor, and Bill Ward were especially helpful with information on plants included in this edition.

I live a seamless life with work and home and play intricately interconnected. The Cibolo Nature Center, where I work, is a remarkable community of dedication, love, and generosity focused on conserving our natural environment. It has given me a place to be creative and supported much of the time spent on this project. I am thankful every day to the nature center's co-founders, Carolyn Chipman-Evans and Brent Evans.

My children, Sarah and Joel, inspire and challenge me. They have grown to believe that my obsession with native plants, birds, bugs, lizards, snakes, mammals, and all things ecological is only slightly abnormal and barely even embarrassing.

I am especially grateful to my husband, Jerry McFarlen, who first chose to live in the Texas Hill Country and continues to share my interest in the native woody plants that contribute so much to the landscape of our lives.

Trees, Shrubs,

and Vines

of the

Texas Hill Country

Map of the Texas Hill Country

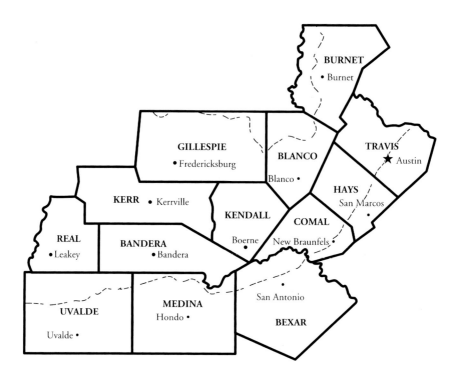

This book is a guide to one hundred Texas Hill Country plants that occur naturally in the Balcones Canyonlands or Hill Country of Central Texas, a geographically unique area adjacent to and west of the Balcones Escarpment. As shown in the map by a dotted line, the area covered by this book includes all of Kendall, Bandera, Real, and Kerr counties; much of Gillespie, Blanco, Burnet, Travis, Hays, and Comal counties; as well as northern Uvalde, Medina, and Bexar counties.

INTRODUCTION TO THE
TEXAS HILL COUNTRY

The Texas Hill Country is a region of exceptional natural beauty. The landscape is well known for its rocky, limestone hills and steep ravines carved by sparkling, spring-fed streams. This rugged geology has nourished abundant, complex native plant communities that give the area its unique character cherished by settlers past and present.

Geology

During the Early Cretaceous period (about 130 to 90 million years ago), what is now Central Texas was on the edge of the ancestral Gulf of Mexico. Many different kinds of marine organisms lived and died here, leaving behind shells and other calcium carbonate parts. These remains eventually disintegrated to produce many layers of calcium carbonate sediment. Over time these sediments turned into layers of limestone. For the last 40 million years, the region has been above sea level. During this time, continuous erosion has stripped off the upper-deposit layers, revealing the older Glen Rose and Edwards limestones. About 20 million years ago, the Balcones Fault system developed along a line running northeast to southwest through Austin, San Marcos, and New Braunfels and north of San Antonio and Uvalde. The land to the east and south of the fault line slipped downward along a series of parallel breaks. To the north, the Texas Hill Country grades gradually to broad valleys with gentle rounded hills.

Native plant communities growing on soil derived from a Glen Rose outcrop may be different from those growing on Edwards soils. Even different parts of each formation support different plants because the variations in composition and texture of the rocks affect soil thickness, moisture, and drainage.

Soils

Although variable throughout the region, Texas Hill Country soil is typically shallow, alkaline, and unsuited to cultivated crops. Limiting features
are rockiness, a shallow root zone, and low water availability. The limestone hills and slopes are covered with a thin, alkaline soil layer with
limited fertility; seeps are common after heavy rainfall.

River bottomland is different. It is usually silty-clay-loam up to forty
inches deep. Although moderately alkaline, Texas Hill Country bottomland
soil has high natural fertility. River valleys may be flooded for a short period
during heavy rainfall. These areas have been, and some continue to be,
used for grain sorghum, oats, wheat, and annual and perennial hay crops.

Topography

Texas Hill Country elevations range from about one thousand to twenty-
five hundred feet above sea level. Streams run south or southeast toward
the Gulf of Mexico. Along the high gradient portion of the Balcones
Escarpment from Austin to San Antonio, the land is dissected with steep-
sided canyons. Here the water commonly runs three hundred to four hundred feet lower than the surrounding ridges. Major permanent streams are
the Frio, Sabinal, Medina, Guadalupe, and Blanco rivers. The Texas Hill
Country also has a number of springs that are an important water source
for many plants and human communities, including New Braunfels and
San Marcos.

Climate

Throughout the area, daily summer temperatures range from the low seven-
ties to the high nineties, with at least a few summer days over one hundred
degrees Fahrenheit. In the winter, temperatures commonly vary between
the mid-thirties to the mid-sixties. The first frost is often in November, and
the last frost, in early March. Thus, the Texas Hill Country growing season is
about 250 days.

Mean annual precipitation is about thirty inches. Rainfall peaks semi-
annually in May–June and September. The source of most Texas Hill Country
precipitation is moisture-laden air, including hurricanes, moving north from
the Gulf of Mexico. The average annual rainfall increases from southwest
to northeast. Little regular rainfall in the summer and high temperatures

produce high evapotranspiration rates. Periodic droughts place regular desiccation stress on all plants. "Gully-washer" storms of twenty to thirty inches in twenty-four hours are irregular but not uncommon. The resulting torrential floods routinely cause severe erosion and property loss along normally small, peaceful streams.

Major Plant Communities

The Texas Hill Country is a mix of evergreen savanna, upland deciduous, and lowland riparian plant communities. Although natural local plant community variations are not well documented, north- and east-facing slopes are consistently cooler and wetter than south- and west-facing slopes. The cooler, wetter locations, mostly canyons, support a diverse mix of deciduous trees, including Uvalde bigtooth maple, black cherry, black walnut, Texas ash, live oak, and cedar elm.

Higher and drier, west- and southwest-facing slopes are mostly evergreen and less varied. Here Ashe juniper and live oak are the dominant trees, and mountain laurel, agarita, evergreen sumac, and Texas persimmon are common shrubs or small trees. In many places, these areas have become overgrown with dense "cedar thickets" where Ashe juniper is by far the dominant plant.

Bottomland plant communities consistently have a substantial mix of understory plants. On seasonal creeks, live oak, hackberry, cedar elm, possumhaw, elbow bush, aromatic sumac, Carolina buckthorn, and greenbrier can make dense, impenetrable thickets. In river bottomlands where a consistent source of water is present, we see an overstory of bald cypress, pecan, American sycamore, sugar hackberry, American elm, cottonwood, and black willow. Springs and river bottomlands also support more water-dependent understory shrubs, such as elderberry, buttonbush, rough leaf dogwood, Turk's cap, spicebush, bush palmetto, trumpet creeper, and mustang grape.

The Past

During recent history, plant communities have been greatly altered by humans. For centuries before European settlers arrived, Native Americans roamed these hills and burned the prairie grasses, attracting buffalo to the lush, new green growth.

In the early 1700s, the region we know as the Texas Hill Country vista was called Lomeria Grande, or "great hills." This old name described a mysterious and little-known place inhabited by Apache, who were feared and avoided by foreign travelers. By the mid-1800s, when the Native Americans had been subdued and the land explored and tamed, the current, much-reduced name came into common use.

At that time, although parts of this region were barren limestone slopes and some plateaus supported no more than a few stunted trees, much of the land was covered by a rich variety of abundant trees, shrubs, tall grasses, and wildflowers. Travelers described seeing lush, cypress-lined streams and narrow riparian pecan bottoms, dense post oak forests, a few gigantic elms, fertile mesquite prairies, beautiful grass-covered valleys, scattered live oaks, densely wooded valleys, formidable hills covered with shrubbery, rough and brushy country, slopes covered with impenetrable thickets of cedar trees, a considerable amount of cedar timber, heavily forested creek banks, an abundance of cedar and various types of oak scattered about in groups, and splendid pockets of tallgrass prairies strewn with brilliant wildflowers.

What happened to the virgin timber?
Early settlers were interested in the trees primarily as timber for lumber. Tall, straight trees were especially useful in building early log cabins. One constructed near Waring and now on the Y-O Ranch is made entirely of elm logs. Some cedar trees were described as stately with uniform spreading crowns and straight trunks to twenty-five feet tall. Because of its durability, the wood of these trees was described by one early New Braunfels settler to be preferred above all others for building houses and fences.

By the 1860s, the huge, virgin cypress trees that lined permanent creeks and rivers of the Hill Country were nearly all cleared for their lumber. Because of cypress wood's natural resistance to dampness, it was especially valuable in shingle making. Kerrville and Kerr counties were founded in 1852 by a shingle maker, Joshua David Brown. Thus, in the Hill Country, as in the rest of North America, the oldest and largest trees were eliminated long ago.

Farm and ranching operations by the European immigrants had a further deleterious impact on native plant communities. Settlers cleared fields

American smoke tree.

and removed unwanted species from land suitable for plowing. Grazing by goats, sheep, and cattle greatly reduced or eliminated especially nutritious species from the landscape. In many areas of the Hill Country, heavy grazing by these animals continues to the present day. Thus, the impact of immigrants has had a far greater impact on Texas Hill Country native plant communities than anything that came before their arrival. None of the virgin wilderness that survived in the Lomeria Grande until the 1850s remains today.

The Present
What exactly are native trees and shrubs?

Because of the great changes in the landscape that followed the initial arrival of European settlers, we consider Texas Hill Country native plants to be those that were present before settlers first immigrated to the area. Nonnative or exotic species found in the Texas Hill Country, such as Bermuda grass and chinaberry trees, have been brought here either accidentally or intentionally by settlers since the 1800s.

How does population growth affect native plants?

Today, reduction of native plant communities in the Texas Hill Country continues as the area experiences increasing growth and an unprecedented construction boom. Large-scale landowners are now clearing their land and subdividing it into small-acreage parcels at a phenomenal rate.

Many new residents move here to enjoy the natural beauty and serenity of the region only to clear away all native growth that remains beneath the oaks. Unaware of the advantages in protecting native landscape, new home builders often remove valuable small- to midsize trees and shrubs from wide areas around their homesites. Unfamiliar with the unique, demanding soil and weather conditions, residents new to the Texas Hill Country can waste thousands of dollars with expensive and often unsuitable landscape plants that cannot survive the alkaline soil or hot, dry weather conditions of the region.

Unaware of what is a healthy Texas Hill Country landscape, many well-intentioned new landowners set about reproducing the starved settings they see on the overgrazed land all around us. Thus, the damage begun by ranchers who eked out a meager living on the land is continued by owners who have inadequate knowledge of the landscape and who have no financial pressure to abuse their land.

The Future

Why protect native trees, shrubs, and vines?

Texans love their land. Some worship the grand Texas vistas from afar and never develop a close tie to any element—hill country, desert, prairie, or beach. Others attempt to dominate a small piece and transform it into a mental picture they have of someplace else. But most of us wish to live on our land and love it day by day, enjoying the daily pleasures of our unique place on earth.

This book is intended to help Texas Hill Country residents recognize and protect our great natural heritage. By learning to appreciate and preserve the rich variety of native trees and shrubs in our environment, we can maintain the beautiful landscape we love and reap many other practical benefits in the process.

The Benefits of Native Trees and Shrubs

The native plants of the Texas Hill Country attract, shelter, and feed color-ful butterflies, delightful songbirds, deer, and many other forms of wildlife. They provide attractive, low-maintenance landscaping and help save money, reduce pollution, and conserve water and energy. With careful manage-ment of adequate acreage, natural vegetation can supply high-quality and dependable browse for livestock, such as cattle, goats, sheep, and horses.

Cover for Wildlife
Shrubs with low-growing branches and foliage provide important cover for insects, ground-dwelling mammals, and many birds that live on or near the ground. Good cover allows them to escape from predators, find protection from wind and rain, build a nest or hide a den, and have a place to perch during the day or roost at night.

Butterflies, songbirds, roadrunners, hummingbirds, turkeys, quail, deer,

Shrubs such as this possumhaw provide food and cover for many creatures, including this rough green snake.

foxes, rabbit, coyotes, and bobcats are among the wild creatures that need the good cover provided by native shrubs in order to survive. Masses of deciduous shrubs are especially important protection from predators for young, inexperienced wild creatures during the spring and summer. During winter months when many plants are without leaves, native evergreen trees and shrubs provide essential protection from predators and severe weather. Holes in imperfect, dead, or dying trees give shelter and nest sites to many wild creatures.

Insects, which are food for many birds, lay their eggs under the bark of woody plants or in the decomposing debris they produce. Trees with elevated canopies provide cover and nesting places for many birds and some mammals, such as squirrels and ringtail cats, that are specialized to live in their branches. Wild creatures nightly roost well hidden in the branches of native trees, shrubs, and vines.

Food for Wildlife

Vines, shrubs, and trees produce fruit and seed consumed by wildlife throughout the year. Animals and birds eating seed-bearing fruit are the primary means of dispersal and establishment for woody plants.

Generally, big birds eat big fruit (turkeys eat pecans and acorns), and smaller birds eat small fruit (mockingbirds eat dogwood berries). Turkeys, quail, wood ducks, jays, crows, mockingbirds, thrashers, robins, bluebirds, waxwings, orioles, tanagers, cardinals, buntings, grosbeaks, towhees, and some sparrows are the most common birds that eat the fruit or seed of trees and shrubs in the Hill Country. Throughout the spring and summer, butterflies and hummingbirds drink nectar from the blossoms of native flowering trees and shrubs.

Wrens, warblers, and vireos are among the many insect-eating birds that depend on the myriad insects living on native trees and shrubs. Butterflies prefer certain nectar plants and lay their eggs on specific plants that their caterpillars must eat in order to survive. The caterpillars in turn find food and safety among the leaves of these plants.

Opossums, raccoon, ringtail cats, foxes, coyotes, squirrels, jackrabbits,

Tree holes, such as the one in this pecan tree, provide shelter and nest sites.

A gray treefrog is camouflaged on tree bark.

cottontails, javelinas, mice, and rats are the most common small mammals that eat the fruit or seed of native trees and shrubs in the Hill Country. In addition, deer and other mammals browse the leaves and tender young twigs of many shrubs and small trees.

An Attractive and Durable Landscape

The best landscaping in the Texas Hill Country is created for maximum beauty and durability. The plants must be tolerant of drought, summer heat, and winter cold. Although they are often overlooked, native Texas Hill Country trees, shrubs, and woody vines, which have passed the test of time, are naturals for this tough job. We are blessed with an abundance of handsome species; in fact, some of the state's most attractive plants grow here on the poorest rocky limestone soil.

The easiest approach to successful landscaping is to begin with an unspoiled natural landscape and enhance its natural charm with the addition of a few colorful native plants, judicious pruning, and occasional mowing. Many of us, however, will buy or already own a home landscaped with a smooth, green lawn, clipped hedges, and a few isolated flower beds. Through lack of knowledge, we or the previous owner probably selected plants that provide little fragrance, color, texture, or variety. Many common landscape plants are not well adapted to Hill Country soil, rainfall, or temperatures and therefore require exorbitant amounts of water, time, and effort to maintain.

You may own or might purchase land that has been heavily overgrazed and is in need of rest, rehabilitation, and careful management to return to its natural variety and charm. Look at your land as well as neighboring wild areas to learn about the variety of trees, shrubs, and vines native to your area. A full year may be necessary to reveal the wealth of useful native plants already established and ready to serve your purposes.

Become your own expert on the plants of this area, or hire a native plant expert to help you evaluate the plants on your land. Doing so could prevent a costly mistake such as the one made by a landowner who accidentally cleared three thousand dollars' worth of Lacey oaks before calling his landscaper. Study your land and its flora. Search especially for vines, shrubs, and small trees that produce colorful or fragrant blossoms, shelter or feed wildlife, and provide shade, privacy, or erosion control. Keep every tree, shrub, and vine that could possibly be useful in your landscape-management plan. A little pruning and the addition of some natives that provide color and variety can make a beautiful and hardy landscape that will provide years of enjoyment with very little maintenance.

Avoid the common mistake of automatically removing all the cedar. This unpopular tree is one of the most important landscape trees in the Hill Country. Cedar provides food and shelter for birds, butterflies, deer, and other wildlife. It is one of the few evergreens that is absolutely drought tolerant and serves as a nurse tree for other plants, such as Texas madrone, American smoke tree, and Texas mountain laurel, whose seedlings commonly start under its canopy. As long as your land is not being overgrazed by wildlife or livestock, cedar is easy to control because it never resprouts from a cut or burned stump. It can be pruned into a small, elegant tree or handsome, round bush; or it can be left as a privacy fence or for erosion control.

Native plants, such as this agarita, serve as host plants for many species of butterflies.

It is not necessary to landscape exclusively with plants that are native to your locale. There are many naturalized imports that are thriving here; however, when adding plants, be careful to select ones that are not invasive and that fit in visually, as well as ones that are hardy and drought tolerant.

Monetary Savings

Native trees and shrubs offer a number of advantages:

- They reduce loss in a natural mix of species should Spanish and live oaks succumb to oak wilt.
- They increase property value. Real estate agents and home buyers typically assign at least 6–20 percent of a property's value to its trees because of the shade they provide and their natural beauty.
- They limit damage or loss from drought and eliminate the expense of replacing expensive plants unsuited to Hill Country soil and weather conditions.
- They reduce landscape watering bills.
- They require fewer pesticides and fertilizers and reduce maintenance costs.
- They provide natural seclusion, eliminating the need to build expensive privacy fences.
- They pose a reduced threat to building foundations because they require less water.

Water Conservation

Well-established native trees and shrubs remain dormant during extensive dry periods and can survive without supplemental watering. Their leaves, bark, and the vines, lichens, and mosses that grow on them catch and retain rainwater for slower movement down and into the soil. A healthy growth of native trees and shrubs covers the ground with shade and natural mulch, which slow the inevitable rise in air and soil temperature and consequent drying of the soil. Thus, tree-shaded lawns do not have to be watered as often.

Energy Conservation

Native trees shading a west-facing wall lower summer temperatures more than 20 percent. Shade also reduces heat reflected by concrete by as much as 50 percent. Leaving trees and shrubs on a northern exposure provides a windbreak that reduces winter winds and lowers heating bills up to 30 percent. A stand of native trees and shrubs provides natural air conditioning by emitting moisture from their leaves. Evaporation of this moisture cools the air under the canopy of a tree or shrub by six to eight degrees.

Reduced Pollution

Trees and shrubs clean the air by removing pollutants such as ozone, sulfur dioxide, nitrogen dioxide, and carbon dioxide and replacing carbon dioxide with oxygen. In a year, one acre of thicket will absorb all the carbon dioxide produced by a car driven twenty-six thousand miles. In addition, trees and shrubbery can trap and remove particles from the air and fill it with their own fragrance. Especially in dense stands, the leaves, bark, and branches of woody vegetation help to scatter sound. Plants also filter and purify surface water, moderate flooding, and slow the movement of rainwater, thus preventing soil loss through erosion.

Woody Plants and White-tailed Deer

Why does the Texas Hill Country have deer overpopulation?

As with all wild animal populations, a white-tailed deer population's size will normally and naturally rise and fall in unending cycles of growth and decline. Several factors contribute to the dynamics of population change. Death rate and emigration reduce population size. Birth rate and immigration represent a population's tendency to increase. These factors, enhancing or diminishing a population, are in turn dependent on the presence of predators and quality of the habitat or on the environmental factors of food, water, and cover.

Before the 1960s, Hill Country white-tailed deer populations were held in check through a high death rate from parasites and large predators, such as coyotes and cougars. Today, the predators of the past have been replaced by humans and regulated seasonal hunting.

The most deadly parasite for white-tailed deer in the Hill Country used to be the screwworm fly, which would lay its eggs on newborn fawns under the skin in the area of the umbilical cord attachment. When the larvae hatched, they would eat the tender flesh of the fawn, causing a serious wound, infection, and an ugly death. In the 1960s the screwworm fly, also a major parasite on cattle, was eradicated by the release of sterile male flies. The demise of this parasite and the removal of natural predators have been a boon to both cattle ranchers and white-tailed deer and a bust for native plant diversity.

What plants do deer eat?
In a good year with plenty of rain, white-tailed deer in sustainable habitat may live on forbs (broad-leaved plants commonly called wildflowers or weeds) in spring and summer. As forbs become less available in the late summer and fall, deer shift to browse (leaves and twigs of woody or shrubby plants), which is usually lower in protein content than the forbs. White-tailed deer are physically able to browse on leaves of trees and shrubs within three to four feet of the ground.

Another type of food produced by woody trees and shrubs is mast (the fruit, acorns, and other seed from these plants). Deer consume mast in the fall and early winter, but mast production in some years is very low, forcing the animals to depend more heavily on browse. White-tailed deer eat only a small amount of very young grass shoots in the early spring. Thus, high deer density does not have a serious impact on grasses growing in the Texas Hill Country.

What are the signs of deer overpopulation?
In the Hill Country, signs that the deer population is higher than the land can support are everywhere. Perhaps the most common sign is the fact that we nearly always ask if the deer will eat it before buying a new landscape plant. Other signs include:

1. A distinct browse line is a definite sign of deer overpopulation. Look for a line about four feet from the ground. Above the browse line are lots of leaves and normal plant growth. Below the line are no leaves or new plant growth because everything is eaten by the deer.

2. Another sign of deer overpopulation is a mass of tiny seedlings growing around a mature tree and no young trees or saplings at all. Without saplings, when the mature trees reach the end of their life span, there will be no other trees to replace them.

3. In areas where deer density is especially high, individual plants are stunted and have small clusters of miniature leaves and no slender branches. Because they are browsed repeatedly, these plants grow only one to three feet tall and will never mature and reproduce as long as the deer are eating them.

What are the consequences of deer overpopulation?
With many more deer on our land than it can sustain, day after day, week after week, month after month, and year after year these hungry browsers are consuming plant species that have defined our ecoregion for hundreds, if not thousands of years. A tree population dies slowly, at a rate so drawn out that we can miss what is happening even though we are present to bear witness. Many native plants preferred by deer are disappearing, while the least nutritious and most unpalatable native species like cedar, mountain laurel, and persimmon are increasing.

Deer overpopulation also means that deer in the backyard and pasture are hungrier, smaller, thinner, and less healthy than they should be. It also means that bucks produce racks that are smaller and in other ways inferior.

What are the signs of good deer management?
When landowners, managers, and hunters see themselves as conservationists, native plant diversity, deer, and all wildlife benefit. Well-managed land will have an abundance of forb, tree, shrub, and vine species. Low branches on trees and shrubs will be leafy and plentiful. According to research conducted at Texas Parks and Wildlife's Kerr Wildlife Management Area, Hill Country white-tailed deer prefer elm, sugar hackberry, Carolina buckthorn, Eve's necklace, plum, madrone, mulberry, and Spanish oak over all other native trees. Where you find young plants of these species, the deer density is sustainable and the deer living in this area will be getting appropriate nutrition.

Browse plants moderately preferred by white-tailed deer are even more important to deer than preferred species because the less popular ones are usually in greater supply. They include the sumacs, post oak, blue oak, redbud, black cherry, possumhaw, and netleaf hackberry. Poison ivy, snailseed vine, clematis, grape, and Virginia creeper are vines also in this category. In the Texas Hill Country, these moderately preferred plant species will be present where appropriate soil and climate conditions exist.

Deer density statistics

Wildlife biologists report that in the Texas Hill Country region of the Edwards Plateau, a white-tailed deer density of one deer per twenty-five to thirty acres is sustainable for a typical healthy landscape that is a mixture of open grassland and treed areas, including cedar thickets and low shrubs.

The annual Texas Parks and Wildlife deer census shows that the Hill Country has an average of about one deer per five to ten acres. In some areas this density is much higher. For example, Fair Oaks Ranch (in northern Bexar, southern Kendall, and western Comal counties) has about one deer per three acres. This extremely high density is common in suburban communities and small towns throughout our region.

Am I part of the problem or part of the solution?

We love the deer, but do we prefer white-tailed deer over all other wildlife? Are we willing to witness the slow decline of other native wildlife and plant species? Do we want our actions to promote the inevitable loss of a piece of our natural heritage? Are we willing to allow smaller and less healthy deer to be a standard in our area? If the answers to any or all of these questions are no, then we need to figure out how to stop the deer overpopulation crisis.

What works, and what doesn't work?

DO NOT FEED THE DEER!

Supplemental feed can increase deer reproductive rates and intensify problems of deer overabundance. Studies of radio-collared deer in Hollywood Park show that deer concentrate around houses that provide extra food. Concentrating deer in small areas maximizes damage to landscape plants and increases the risk of disease and parasite transmission between herd members. Fed deer also become less fearful of people, increasing the risk of vehicle collisions and aggressive behavior toward humans. The solution to deer overpopulation begins with one simple rule: DO NOT FEED THE DEER. Deer also eat at bird feeders. Either keep backyard bird feeders above deer reach or bring them inside at night.

HUNTING

The Texas Parks and Wildlife Department (TPWD) is the state agency charged with white-tailed deer management. Because TPWD regulates deer hunting, it might seem obvious that the agency should add days to the season and/or increase the annual bag limit per license. But these solutions have been put into effect with no significant reduction in deer densities. In the future, we may look to TPWD for further leadership in addressing this problem. Deer overpopulation requires multiple approaches. We all can help in our own way.

ROUTINE URBAN TRAP AND REMOVAL

In urban and suburban towns, like Hollywood Park and Fair Oaks Ranch, deer hunting is unsafe and prohibited. For deer overpopulation control in these settings, a city or community can conduct routine trapping and removal. To be effective, deer trapping and removal must be a long-term, population maintenance program.

CONTRACEPTION

Towns and suburbs with high deer densities are not confined areas with a known number of identifiable deer that can be counted, caught, and treated. Controlling numbers by contraception requires an annual booster administered to each animal by rifle. Because of the obvious difficulties and exceptionally high cost, birth control as a method of reducing deer population is not yet a practical solution.

ANNUAL DEER HARVEST

To control deer population in the Hill Country, where there are so many more animals present than the food supply can support, **we need to remove two out of every three deer!** Such a drastic reduction will take many years, so now is the time to start. Landowners who understand deer overpopulation and its consequences must intensify annual deer hunting on their property.

DOE HUNTING

Trophy buck hunting is imbedded in deer hunter psychology and values. Years of trophy buck hunting have produced a white-tailed deer population that has five times more does than bucks. This is a doe-to-buck ratio of 5:1. A normal sex ratio would be 1:1. In such an imbalanced population, doe harvesting is a key to population management. Annual removal of large numbers of does is essential to reducing density and improving deer health and size.

CONSERVATION GARDENING

Not everyone is temperamentally suited to be a deer hunter. If you are a gardener and not a hunter, native plant propagation and protection might be for you. Are you landscaping with plants the deer love or hate? Conservation gardening calls for using the native plants that deer love. By landscaping with these "priority species" that are in decline because of deer overpopulation, your garden will increase native plant diversity.

TEXAS HILL COUNTRY "PRIORITY PLANTS"

Do you know a priority native plant when you see it? To be an effective conservation gardener, get to know the priority species listed here. These are the ones that are now uncommon because they are the favorite forage of white-tailed deer. Learn to love the plants that deer love, find them, plant them, and protect them from the deer. Consider shopping for these plants at the native plant nurseries listed at the back of this book. If they are not available at the nurseries, ask for them! Encourage your favorite local nursery to propagate them. Convince your neighbors, friends, and relatives to request and garden with them, too. Create the demand, and commercial growers will make them available.

Some top priority natives are Blanco crabapple, American smoke tree, canyon mock orange, hawthorn, Texas and red mulberry, rusty blackhaw, redroot, mountain mahogany, snowbells, and escarpment black cherry. Bigtooth maple is also a high priority tree and one that is fairly easy to find at local nurseries.

DEER EXCLOSURES

Once planted, priority species must be protected from the deer! If you don't live behind a high deer fence, this means using deer exclosures around the plants. In conservation gardening, we must learn to live with deer exclosures. A handsome wire-fence circle around a lovely tree or cluster of trees and shrubs works well. Deer exclosures can be both creative and conservative. Perhaps in time, it will be common to see attractive exclosures sold at nurseries next to the priority plants.

After deer density is reduced, how quickly will habitat recovery occur?
Where sustained over-browsing has reduced plant cover and diversity,
the natural succession of plant communities and nutrient cycling is
disrupted. Restoration of severely over-browsed habitat is a very slow
process. The cascading effects of plant loss extend to creatures besides
deer, including other mammals, insects, and birds. Although ecosystem
revitalization is possible when deer density is reduced, resurgence of
bird and other animal populations can only occur with the slow return
of understory vegetation.

Priority Plants of the Texas Hill Country

The priority plant designation comes from over twenty-five years of obser-
vation. These are species whose Texas Hill Country populations appear to
be in decline. As priority plants of this region, they deserve special attention and conservation. Those in boldface are "top priority" species because
they either have been scarce for a long time or are now decreasing at an
alarming rate. These "top priority" species should be planted and protected
in native landscapes wherever their survival is likely.

VINES (7)		
Coral Honeysuckle	*Lonicera sempervirens*	sun
Lindheimer's Morning Glory	***Ipomoea lindheimeri***	**part shade**
Bracted Passion Flower	***Passaflora affinis***	**part shade**
Carolina Snailseed	*Cocculus carolinus*	sun–part shade
Trumpet Creeper	*Campsis radicans*	sun
Virginia Creeper	*Parthenocissus quinquefolia*	part shade
White Honeysuckle	*Lonicera albiflora*	sun–part shade
SHRUBS (18)		
Black Dalea	***Dalea frutescens***	**sun**
Bush Palmetto	***Sabal minor***	**shade**
Canyon Mock Orange	***Philadelphus texensis***	**part shade–shade**
Creek Plum	*Prunus rivularis*	sun–part shade

Elbowbush	*Forestiera pubescens*	part shade–shade
False Indigo	***Amorpha fruticosa***	**part shade**
Hawthorn	***Crategus sp.***	**part shade**
Mexican Plum	*Prunus mexicana*	part shade
Pink Mimosa	*Mimosa borealis*	sun
Possumhaw	*Ilex decidua*	sun–part shade
Redroot	*Ceanothus herbaceous*	sun
Rough Leaf Dogwood	*Cornus drummondii*	part shade
Rusty Blackhaw	***Viburnum rufidulum***	**sun–part shade**
Spicebush	***Lindera benzoin***	**part shade**
Sycamore-leaf Snowbell	***Styrax platanifolius***	**part shade–shade**
Texas Kidneywood	*Eysenhardtia texana*	sun
Texas Mulberry	***Morus microphylla***	**part shade**
Witch Hazel	***Hamamelis virginiana***	**shade**
TREES (16)		
American Elm	***Ulmus americana***	**part shade**
American Smoke Tree	***Cotinus obovatus***	**sun**
Blanco Crabapple	***Malus ioensis* var. *texensis***	**part shade**
Bigtooth Maple	***Acer grandidentatum* var. *sinuosum***	**part shade**
Carolina Buckthorn	*Frangula caroliniana*	sun–part shade
Cedar Elm	*Ulmus crassifolia*	sun–part shade
Escarpment Black Cherry	***Prunus serotina* var. *eximia***	**sun–part shade**
Eve's Necklace	*Sophora affinis*	sun–part shade
Red Mulberry	*Morus rubra*	part shade
Slippery Elm	***Ulmus rubra***	**part shade**
Shin Oak	*Quercus sinuate*	sun–part shade
Soapberry	*Sapindus saponaria* var. *drummondii*	sun
Spanish Oak	*Quercus buckleyi*	sun–part shade
Texas Barberry	*Berberis swaseyi*	sun–part shade
Texas Redbud	*Cercis canadensis* var. *texensis*	sun–part shade
Texas Madrone	***Arbutus xalapensis***	**part shade**

Woody Plants and Ranching

Some ranchers regard small trees and shrubs as pests to be eliminated. Woody plants do compete with grasses for water, nutrients, and sunlight; however, browse plants are nutritious and palatable forage, sought out and eaten by deer and livestock. Cedar, mesquite, beebush, and some others are not particularly nutritious or palatable and are avoided by deer and livestock. Consequently, they can increase to highly undesirable levels and create land-management problems. Still, browse plants contribute nutrient cycling, nitrogen fixation, and organic enrichment to the soil. In addition, these plants prevent runoff, increase the amount of water absorbed by the soil, and decrease soil erosion.

Which trees and shrubs are good browse?
Animals eat their favorite plants first and over a modest period of time can eliminate the best species, allowing less desirable ones to increase. This order of plant selection is predictable and allows us to group Texas Hill Country trees and shrubs into four classes according to preference. Forage plants are rated for leaf and twig consumption rather than mast preference. Because of erratic rainfall patterns in the Hill Country, mast is not a reliable food source on which to base range-management decisions. The following lists are the classes of browse preference for the Texas Hill Country trees, shrubs, and woody vines covered in this book.

CLASS I: HIGHLY PREFERRED
Plants are nutritious and palatable food but not usually abundant enough to make a major contribution as deer or livestock forage.
   Bigtooth maple
   Blanco crabapple
   Bush palmetto
   Carolina buckthorn
   Cedar elm
   Eve's necklace
   Kidneywood
   Madrone
   Redroot
   Rusty blackhaw

Spanish oak
Sugar hackberry
Sycamore leaf snowbell
White honeysuckle
Turk's cap

CLASS II: MODERATELY PREFERRED
Plants offer a major contribution to the diet of range animals, but they are heavily impacted where land is overpopulated with deer or livestock.

American smoke tree
Aromatic sumac
Black cherry
Bois d'arc
Carolina snailseed
Evergreen sumac
Greenbrier
Gum bumelia
Mock orange
Mustang grape
Poison ivy
Possumhaw
Post oak
Rough leaf dogwood
Texas redbud
Virginia creeper

CLASS III: EATEN BUT NOT PREFERRED
Plants' nutritional quality is usually less than ideal for browsing animals. The plants may be a major food source, and some are often used for range-management decisions.

Agarita
American beautyberry
Bald cypress
Black dalea
Common buttonbush
Creek plum

Elbow bush
Elderberry
Flameleaf sumac
Huisache
Lacey oak
Live oak
Old man's beard
Pecan
Pink mimosa
Red mulberry
Retama
Sotol
Spicebush
Texas walnut
Tickle tongue
Wafer ash
Western soapberry

CLASS IV: UNDESIRABLE

Plants are consumed only when little other food is available. They create brush problems because they are not eaten by livestock and deer.

Ashe juniper
Beargrass
Black willow
Cenizo
Common beebrush
Dewberry
Lindheimer's silktassel
Mesquite
Mountain laurel
Pale buckeye
Pearl milkweed
Poverty bush
Texas lantana
Texas persimmon
Twist leaf yucca

A fence provides dramatic evidence of an overused landscape.

How much land is necessary for ranching?
Because soil quality and the amount and type of vegetation present in the
Texas Hill Country vary, it is difficult to give an accurate figure for the
number of acres necessary to support livestock. For land that is neither
especially rich bottomland nor a poor upland site covered with dense cedar
thicket, an average number of acres might be thirty per horse, twenty-five
per cow, fifteen per donkey, five per sheep, and four per goat. Of course,
with supplemental feeding, animals can be kept on much smaller parcels
or dry lots, where the trees, shrubs, and grasses will be heavily compro-
mised.

Land that has been overused and abused will need recovery time, and
browse recovery takes longer than grass recovery time. Poor range where
Class III and IV plants show heavy to moderate use will need an initial rest
period of one to three years. Fair rangeland where few Class II plants are
present and Class III plants show moderate use may need stocking reduc-
tions to double acreage per head.

How are browse conditions determined?
Overbrowsing will eventually eliminate desirable trees and shrubs from
pastures, and undesirable species will take over. Moderate browsing will
allow woody plants to remain healthy and reproduce. Moderate browse is
the most efficient use of forage for livestock-management programs, and
"take half, leave half" is a common rule of thumb for grass and browse
management.

The key browse species on which to base livestock-management decisions should be plants common in the pasture that are in the most preferred class represented. Proper use of the dominant Class III species
(often live oak) is a common management practice:

- Light browse: Most twigs and leaves will be untouched.
- Moderate browse: About one-half of the leaves and twigs will be
  eaten. Use an unbrowsed twig from at least five feet above the
  ground for comparison.
- Heavy browse: All small twigs will be eaten, so leaves grow in
  tight clumps on stunted branches.

Clear browse line is a sign of overuse.

Browsing that causes moderate hedging is not harmful to a woody plant and can serve to keep more forage in reach of the browsing animals. Long-term heavy browsing reduces leaf size and twig length and will eventually kill the plants. A browse line develops on trees and large shrubs when heavy browsing removes branches, twigs, and leaves within reach of the animals. Where distinct browse lines occur, forage available to the live-stock has been greatly reduced by overuse. The forage resources are dete-riorating because seedlings never get established.

To develop the best livestock-management plan for your ranch, consult the district conservationist in the Natural Resources Conservation Service office nearest you.

Cedar Management

There are six species of juniper native to Texas, but only one species, *Juniperus ashei,* grows naturally in the Texas Hill Country. It is commonly called Ashe juniper, mountain cedar, cedar, or something much worse.

In 1857, an early Texas traveler named Frederick Law Olmsted wrote a description of what he saw after crossing the Blanco River about halfway between Boerne and Austin: "We pitched our tent at night in a live-oak grove. . . . Behind us were the continuous wooded heights, with a thick screen of cedars; before us, very beautiful prairies, rolling off far to the southward, with the smooth grassed surface, varied here and there by herds of cattle, and little belts, mottes and groups of live oak." This word picture suggests that in the mid-1850s, the stream valleys of the Texas Hill Country were more open than today, with fewer trees and more extensive grasslands, and that the steep slopes were heavily wooded with trees, including cedar.

Why is cedar so hard to control?
Before European settlements and extensive ranching, the spread of cedar was kept in check by wildfire, ignited by lightning and Native American peoples. These fires burned far and wide on lush grass fuels. They were a key element in maintaining the natural plant communities and kept cedar trees limited to locations that did not experience regular fires. With the arrival of Europeans, sheep and cattle ranching increased throughout the Hill Country, and barbed-wire fencing was introduced to control livestock. More and more land was fenced and grazed by sedentary herds. Much of the heavy grass cover was eaten by cattle, fires were less common, and cedar reproduced and spread onto the new, bare landscapes that overgrazing and cessation of natural fires—often coupled with drought—created.

Because previous land use has disturbed the balance in our natural plant communities, today we have far more cedar than many people would like. Because it grows in alkaline soil, through cold and extreme heat, and with very little water, it thrives on our hills and in our canyons.

How do I make a cedar-management plan?
Unfortunately, there is no recommended single, "no-thinking-involved" method to manage cedar. Strategies for successful cedar management must be based on sound information and wise judgment. What should be done depends on the age of cedar growth, soil condition, and land slope and direction, as well as personal land-use goals.

Take your time. Get to know your land through the soles of your boots. Get to know your neighbors, too, and learn what information they have about the history of land use in your area. Talk with your family about what you want from your land. Walk and talk, and look and listen for at least a year. Keep a written record of your observations, thoughts, and conversations about your land. Give yourself time to get to know your land in all seasons. Study your native plants, make an inventory or get one done to determine what grows and what ought to grow, and learn where cedar should occur naturally. Only then are you ready to make a successful plan.

Start by writing both long- and short-term goals. Short-term goals might be accomplished in one year, and long-term goals might be what you want your land to look like in five, ten, or even twenty years. Once your goals are clear, choose the steps necessary to reach those goals.

Cedar management can be overwhelming and can seem an impossible task. Once you have made a plan for the desired condition of your landscape, tackle the cedar in phases. Divide the job into small parcels. Put your cedar-clearing efforts on a rotation cycle. When you make a cedar-clearing schedule, consider your physical and financial constraints. Clearing smaller plots instead of clearing everything at once is less stressful on the environment.

If you own property that has cedar thicket or second-growth cedar, how much you remove will depend on your land-management goals. For example, if you have a cedar-covered hillside with small grass clumps and your goal is to encourage the grass to grow and spread, do not clear-cut. Removing all the overgrown cedar will produce undesirable soil erosion before the existing grass can spread to replace the cedar cover. Instead, cut 50–80 percent of the cedar and leave plenty of slash in contact with the ground to hold the soil until the grass returns naturally. The new grass needs time to produce root systems and ground cover that will blanket the land and catch the rainwater.

After thinning the cedar, rest the land from grazing for at least a year. With normal rainfall, existing grasses will reestablish themselves before they are subjected again to the feet and mouths of livestock. If optimum grass production is your goal and the land is flat or slopes less than twenty degrees, you can clear all the cedar. Before clearing, check to make sure that you still have at least sparse grass clumps as a seed source for re-growth. If not, see the section on reseeding.

Why not get rid of it all?
The Hill Country has a forest ecology that bears closer examination. His-torically, the land supported different combinations of woody and herb-aceous plant species depending on its slope, or aspect, and its exposure—north, south, east, or west.

For example, an east-facing slope on the southwest portion of the Bal-cones Canyonlands might typically have a mix of hardwoods, such as es-carpment black cherry, bigtooth maple, pale buckeye, Carolina buckthorn, and Texas ash. A west-facing slope might have Ashe juniper (mountain cedar), live oak, mountain laurel, gum bumelia, and Texas persimmon. In either case, the healthy forest community has an overstory, midstory, and understory with grass and forb ground cover. This successful combination, which in the Hill Country includes cedar, thrives and protects the soil from erosion in all forested ecosystems.

To many birds and other wildlife, a parklike setting with an expanse of short grass under a monoculture of live oaks, such as one might see in some places in the Hill Country, is poor habitat with little food or shelter. A live oak–short-grass park is an unnatural plant community, artificially maintained.

Because cedar belongs in the natural community of plants in the Hill Country, in most situations, clearing every stick of cedar is unnecessary and not the best choice.

Are there any circumstances in which cedar removal is not advised?
Before removing cedar, look for a browse line under the cedar. This defined line will be at the upper reach of white-tailed deer or goats. It indicates that the property is heavily overpopulated by deer or livestock. Next, check the soil under the cedar for grass or forbs. If you do not find any, the ani-mals have eaten the food supply and seed source down so drastically that

there may be no chance of regrowth. Under these conditions, you have two choices: leave the cedar because it is in a relatively stable community, or exclude all browsing animals and wait a year to see what happens. If no new vegetation appears on which you could base a plan of action, you may want to remove the cedar completely and reseed with native grasses from a commercial supplier.

What are the best chemical, biological, and mechanical methods for cedar removal?

CHEMICAL

Although herbicides should be used only in specific situations, they are an effective, inexpensive, and easy means to kill cedar less than three feet tall. Larger cedar trees must be cut or burned. *Always follow herbicide label directions exactly!*

Be aware that using a chemical includes the risk of killing "non-target" species, contamination of a larger area than intended, and potential problems of which we are now unaware. *Never* use an herbicide to kill cedar anywhere near an oak tree, because oaks are sensitive to herbicides.

FIRE

On rural property with second-growth cedar under five feet tall, fire is recommended after the habitat is assessed and a burn plan, if feasible, is developed by a certified land manager or certified "burn boss." Do not conduct a prescribed burn on old-growth cedar stands because their crown fires can too easily get out of control. If you wish to burn a parcel that is not within a subdivision or city limits, contact your local Cooperative Extension agent or Natural Resources Conservation Service representative. Contact names and numbers are listed in the resources section of this publication.

GOATS

Though not usually recommended, in some circumstances goats can be used to suppress cedar because cedar dies when all its green growth is removed. To clear a pasture with early second-growth cedar at a height accessible to the goats, use a herd of goats pastured during December–February. The disadvantage in this cedar-control method is that goats will

The right nipper is good for small cedar.

eat nearly everything else before they consume the cedar. Because cedar is
low on the goats' preference list, small, nontarget evergreen species such
as live oak and the tender shoots and branches of small deciduous shrubs
and hardwoods will be eaten first.

TOOLS

For small jobs or where adequate human labor is available, tree shears,
chain saws, nippers, and loppers are the recommended tools for cedar removal. Although this method is labor intensive, these tools allow the most
careful selection of the trees to be cut and trees to be saved according to
the plan you have put in place.

   Although bulldozers have sometimes been used when clearing very
large ranches or when making a wide path through a cedar thicket, this
method is not used much any more because it is expensive and disturbs soil
profoundly, aggravates erosion, and destroys everything in the bulldozer's
path. Because of the machine's size and power, it can easily remove desirable plants along with the targeted species. Trees to be saved should be
clearly tagged. Always use an operator who is responsive to your instruc-
tions, and make it a point to be present during the work.

Chaining, a method where a massive chain is dragged across the land between two Caterpillars, is not practiced anymore because chaining destroys all trees indiscriminately.

The hydro-ax is a machine that chews a cedar tree from its top down to the ground. Its drawback is that it can create a mulch pile so deep that nothing will grow there.

Hydraulic shears are usually mounted on the back of a Bobcat and do not disturb soil as other machines do. They can take big and little trees, although there is a limit on the tree diameter they can handle. Do not work on steep slopes where you should not cut cedar anyway, and do not take mature trees.

What do I do with all the mountains of cut cedar?
No matter which tools are used for cedar clearing, you will end up with unwieldy mountains of slash. When clearing cedar from a slope, always leave some slash at the top to slow surface-water flow. For maximum effect, place some branches with trunks uphill and some with trunks downhill.

If you have no plans for a prescribed burn, you can stack cedar slash under hardwood trees. Or if you want a cleaner look, you can put a half-inch layer of cedar mulch on the ground that will shade the soil and lower soil

Slash stacked in contact with the ground will slow runoff.

Cedar mulch retains moisture but must not be too deep.

Tepees made from cedar slash provide good wildlife habitat.

temperature but still allow grass and forbs to grow. The mulch layer will also retain moisture and support more plant regeneration.

Disk or drum chippers are great machines for reducing huge cedar-slash piles into useful mulch chips. They rent locally for $150 per eight-hour day and are safe and easy to use. Most disk chippers will grind up cedar from the smallest twigs up to trees seven inches in diameter. Use the chipper to spread the mulch over a wide area so that it is no deeper than one-half inch. Deeper mulch will smother dormant grass and forb seeds and prevent their regrowth.

You may also want to burn much of your slash. Be sure to check with the county for current burn regulations, and get a certified person to conduct the burn. Remember that nothing will grow for a long time in the soil under a cedar-pile fire, because the fire's intense heat sterilizes the soil. To speed regrowth, rake soil into the burned area.

Consider building a brush pile with some of the cedar slash to create a habitat for birds and wildlife. In open areas, build cedar tepees with branches on the ground and trunks tied together in the air. These tepees will remain good wildlife habitat for at least fifteen years; whereas cedar stacked on the ground, although good for controlling erosion and sheltering seedlings, will compress in a couple years and be useful only to the smallest rodents.

Which kinds of grass seed should be used to reseed?
In most situations, it is unnecessary to spread grass seed in cleared or thinned areas. Enough native grass seed is usually present for the grasses to return on their own. If you do need to reseed an area that has lost its natural seed source, learn which kinds of grasses ought to be seeded, and find a local source of native seed that guarantees its product. Do not plant King Ranch bluestem, which is an invasive exotic species, or any mix that includes it or any other nonnative grass. Be aware that native seed is expensive, so establishing patches that will be a seed source for the larger parcel may be your best choice.

How can cleared, bare soil be protected from erosion?
As you remove the cedar, read your land and look for rills—channels of bare ground eroded by previous runoff events. Place the cedar slash in

windrows, or perpendicular to the slope, over these paths. Leave the windrows one to two years or until the new grass cover is established.

To prevent erosion on very steep slopes, never remove all the cedar. When clearing on lesser grades, leave windrows at the top of each slope. Place the slash in contact with the ground, where it will catch and slow the runoff. Rainwater absorbed here may then seep out slowly at a lower level, where it waters a second plant community.

What do I need to do to protect the trees I want to keep?
When removing cedar, you will encounter hardwoods that should be protected during the massive environmental changes you are engineering. Use orange environmental fencing to cordon off the land within the tree's drip line to avoid drastically altering the environment around any hardwood tree. Spanish oaks are especially sensitive. You will also want to protect mature cedars and other cedars that act as "nurse trees," where plants that are especially vulnerable to deer browse are sheltered within their branches. Canyon mock orange, American smoke tree, madrone, and sycamore leaf snowbell are a few that commonly grow within the protection of mountain cedar.

Does cedar "hog" water?
Cedar, like any tree, needs a lot of water to live, but a cedar tree does not hog water. Cedar retains and uses its water very efficiently. This efficiency is possible because cedars have small leaves covered with a waxy coating that limits transpiration or water loss. Conversely, a tree such as sycamore that has big, thin leaves with a large surface area might be considered a water guzzler because of the high rate of transpiration or water loss through its leaves. For this reason, sycamores grow only along streams and lakes or other places where water is plentiful.

Cedar thickets create a closed canopy whose dense overhead cover can sometimes inhibit or slow the amount of precipitation that reaches the ground. However, this negative characteristic can also be a positive one on steep slopes that are most subject to erosion. A cedar brake in a steep-sided canyon will reduce runoff and erosion. In addition, the precipitation that makes its way more slowly down to the ground on these slopes will be more likely to percolate into the soil.

Cedars can serve as "nurse trees" for other native species.

However water-efficient it is, mountain cedar does use water, and the large, unnatural monocultures of cedar that have spread across much of the Texas Hill Country consume significant amounts of water. The water used by these cedar trees is not available to other plants, surface streams, or underground aquifers. When large, heavy stands of cedar are removed or thinned, rainwater is made available to grasses, shrubs, and other trees as well as to surface and groundwater supplies. Everything we do that stops rainwater runoff and increases its infiltration into the soil helps either the local habitat or the groundwater supply. For example, even a backyard gardener can help by placing a thin (no deeper than one-half inch) layer of cedar mulch on soil to enhance rainwater absorption. This layer of mulch will also help grass and forb seeds germinate and grow into an absorbent carpet that protects the soil from erosion, reduces evaporation, and increases infiltration.

It is not necessary to remove all the cedar from your land to increase surface and groundwater supplies. Clearing in a way that prevents erosion, opens a closed canopy, and increases the amount of water absorbed by the soil will benefit nearby streams and help recharge the aquifer.

How does cedar affect the diversity of native plant communities?
A cedar thicket probably contains more other plant species than most people would expect, but many species will not thrive in the heavy shade made by a dense cedar thicket. Thinning a thick cedar brake will allow sunlight to reach the understory shrubs, forbs, and grasses. After you remove or thin cedar, be patient. Wait before spending money on new plants or seed. Give the existing plants an opportunity to thrive in the new light, and let dormant seeds germinate. You may be surprised at how many species are present. A prescribed burn is also very effective in stimulating germination of seeds long dormant and available to renew the plant community. (Refer to the section on prescribed burns.)

How can cedar management promote wildlife?
Cedar can be important cover in the winter when all animals and birds need shelter from the winter wind. A thick, second-growth cedar tree with heavy branches covered with leaves all the way to the ground will be better cover than a slender tree with branches only at the top.

Many birds eat cedar "berries" (the fruit of Ashe juniper is really a cone that looks like a berry). The western scrub-jay is a species whose numbers have been declining in recent years. This large jay depends on cedar for its nest and the cedar berries for its food. The endangered golden-cheeked warbler feeds on insects that live among the leaves and branches of the hardwood trees that are commonly mixed with cedar in east- or north-facing canyons. This endemic species, exclusive to the Texas Hill Country,

Greg Lasley

Western scrub-jays live and nest in cedar.

nests in the sheltered canyons of the Edwards Plateau, where it builds its nest using slender strips of bark picked off older cedar trees.

Areas of mixed plant species will feed and provide nest sites for breeding, migratory, and resident birds. For example, thrashers, thrush, towhees, and wrens thrive in old second-growth cedar with understory for shelter and nesting. Thus, in assessing second growth, leave trees that provide the most shelter for these birds and other wildlife. When choosing which cedar trees to keep and which to clear, remove trees with straight trunks and leave multitrunk trees for perches and cover. When clearing young second-growth cedar, you might want to leave a few thick, round cedar bushes that can be good winter cover for songbirds.

Like all wildlife, deer need food, water, and cover. They will eat cedar if they are starving, but cedar does not provide adequate nutrition for a healthy animal. Cedar does provide good cover for deer, which should be taken into account when removing cedar from your land.

Because wildlife depends on plants for food and shelter, plant communities are an important element in wildlife-management strategies. To

A thick, round cedar bush provides cover for wildlife.

maximize wildlife opportunities on your land, plan for a mosaic of habitats, appropriate to the size and location of your property, that provide
different kinds of cover and food. Sometimes, just cutting a path or a road
will afford a vantage point for identifying areas to keep or change. This also
creates an edge, a transitional area, and a habitat that may nurture species
that do not find the necessary food or shelter in a dense cedar brake.

How can I create habitat for golden-cheeked warblers?
These birds are summer residents that winter in southern Mexico and Central America and nest only on the Edwards Plateau. Thus, the habitat you
supply will be of special importance. If you have shaded canyons that support mature deciduous woodlands, you may have golden-cheeked warbler
habitat. These places are cooler than south- and west-facing canyons and
have a higher percentage of hardwood trees, where the golden-cheeked
warblers tend to build their nests.

To change a cedar-infested canyon into warbler habitat, do not remove more than 35 percent of the total tree canopy. You can remove the trees that are straight and less than ten feet tall and use them as fence poles, but remember, these birds need the bark of mature cedar trees to build their nests.

Healthy Streams and Woody Plants

Riparian refers to the area along a stream or around a pond that is influenced by the body of water. Where the banks are steep, the riparian zone is narrow. Where the banks are lower, the riparian zone is wide. Vegetation in this area is important to the stability and quality of the stream or pond. We know these areas to be naturally lush greenbelts. The riparian zones are probably the most important wildlife habitats in the Texas Hill Country.

Riparian zones are very popular. Everyone wants a piece of the stream: livestock, birds, wildlife, developers, purchasers, anglers, and boaters. When planning for land use in a riparian zone, we must always remember that the area is in constant change. It will never remain the same from generation to generation or even year to year. On the other hand, a well-managed and healthy riparian zone is in dynamic equilibrium and will remain in a steady state within predictable parameters.

In low-water years, the stream will be narrow and meandering. With high water, the stream will be wider and straighter. As floods come and go, the stream will erode material from one place and deposit it as new material in another place. Depositions at first will be raw wounds without any vegetation. Then the pioneer plants, black willow, switchgrass, poverty bush, and sycamore, move in and grow wide, deep root systems that hold the soil and heal the wound.

It is necessary to understand that our pioneer riparian species are here only because the Texas Hill Country has intermittent but regular major floods creating the wounds that are these plants' natural habitat—open, water-saturated soil. Pioneer species are emergency healers of the natural world, similar to EMS technicians that rush to the scene of an accident. Just as we have EMS because accidents always happen, nature has healer plants because floods always happen.

How do I know if my stream is healthy or not?

Consider the stream and its riparian zone as a functioning system that fulfills certain natural requirements in the environment. A healthy, functioning stream system accomplishes the following, resulting in improved water quality; varied stream conditions, including pools, riffles, and runs; habitat for fish and wildlife; and greater biodiversity:

- Dissipates the energy of the water flowing down its channel and reduces downstream flooding
- Reduces erosion
- Filters out sediment carried by the water
- Captures some of the material carried by the stream
- Holds and slowly releases water to the stream
- Improves floodplain development
- Aids groundwater recharge
- Develops dense root masses that will stabilize the banks

A stream that has been stripped of its vegetation can recover more rapidly than dry, upland areas because the available water promotes faster plant growth. Conversely, a stream is affected by what is happening on *all* the land in its watershed. You may do all the "right" things on your land and still have erosion if the land upstream is being overgrazed or cleared and is covered with the impermeable ground cover of development.

What are the benefits of natural vegetation?

It is always best to prevent excessive runoff and erosion before they happen by maintaining stable vegetation with little bare ground. The benefits of a healthy riparian zone with natural vegetation are many:

- Plants with extensive root systems hold the soil and prevent erosion.
- Natural vegetation cleans the water, providing high-quality drinking water for wildlife and humans.
- Shade from dense trees and shrubs cools the water and creates better aquatic habitat.
- Natural vegetation on a stream is a wildlife corridor critical to many species in neighboring ecosystems.
- Better rainwater infiltration through the system increases aquifer recharge.

A healthy stream functions as a natural system, improving water quality and increasing biodiversity.

An at-risk stream can recover in the right conditions.

- Plants act like a sponge, holding and then slowly releasing water, creating consistent downstream flow.

A stream may be functioning well on a day-to-day basis but still be at risk. A common example is a stream that has been stripped clear of both ground cover and understory by generations of overgrazing. When the livestock is removed and the land rested for a year, the grasses and annual forbs will grow back fairly quickly and create a ground cover. In the next few years, perennials will move in and improve the root systems holding the soil; however, until the naturally occurring shrubs and small trees return, the system is not yet able to function at full capacity.

Through the years, as more and more vegetation matures to trap sediment carried in by small regular floods, new soil will accumulate and rebuild banks that have been cut away. Eventually, the new bank will be covered with vegetation and held in place by extensive root systems that protect the stream even in a moderate to large flood.

A stream that is stripped of its vegetation (opposite) no longer functions properly.

In places where a healthy, functioning stream includes a mass of under-brush, access to the stream may be limited and in conflict with intended land use. This problem can be solved by developing limited-access points. For aesthetics or human use, create a favorite "picnic area" for family and friends. For ranch management, isolate a restricted area where the live-stock may continue to have access to the stream.

How concerned should I be about floods?

Do not concern yourself with the so-called five-hundred-year floods. Dam-age is inevitable. Concentrate instead on managing your stream for opti-mum function during the much more frequent bank-full floods. You may see problem erosion after a big flood, but if your stream is healthy and in proper functioning condition, it will use the regular smaller floods to repair itself. Practice ecological patience, and allow nature to do its work in its own time. With patient management practices, your stream will have time to restore itself before the next huge flood.

How should I inspect my stream?

You should regularly inspect your stream and its surroundings. Conduct annual inspections of your stream channel. Take regular photographs from fixed points, and use them for comparison. Always document floods with written and photographic records. Monitor a wide area of the land that sheds water into the stream, and evaluate the ground cover, look-ing for only a little bare ground between frequent tall-grass clumps. After a rainstorm, check for sheeting across the land surface, where pieces of plants will be moved to line up in irregular slender patterns. Sheeting is an indication of excessive runoff, active erosion, and soil loss. At the mouth of a tributary, check for excessive sand, gravel, or rock deposits that may indi-cate a problem upstream in the watershed.

How do I improve the health of my stream?

When you notice streamside damage, the first step is to find the source of the problem. Erosion occurs because of excessive runoff from somewhere upstream. Identify the source by considering the presence of newly cleared land for homesites or other development, new roads, overgrazing, clearing activity, or any other disturbance of natural vegetation.

Sheeting is caused by inadequate ground cover and excessive runoff.

Anything that will increase the rate at which rainwater is absorbed by the soil, instead of becoming immediate and rapid runoff into the stream, will help control erosion. Consider some of the following solutions:

- Fence livestock away from the stream so plants will regrow.
- Limit livestock to a small area of the stream if watering is required.
- Remove livestock altogether, or establish a new grazing system that will rest pastures on a regular basis.
- Let most of the riparian zone return to natural vegetation, mowing only a favorite picnic area.
- Reseed with native seed if necessary, as after mechanical repair of land.
- Terrace or contour to diminish rapid runoff, but never change the natural meander of a stream.
- Work with upstream owners on riparian management education and cooperative management practices.

The stream is a dynamic system surviving flood and drought for generations and beyond. Wise land managers today understand their streams as ever-changing ecosystems that are, or should be, in a state of dynamic equilibrium. The land manager's challenge is to understand what is normal in this dynamic system and be able to distinguish it from the abnormal.

When something abnormal happens, its cause must be located, and the cause of a riparian problem will not be found at the location of the problem. We have to look upstream where we may not have control. A development with clearing and impermeable ground cover may be sending large quantities of water downstream all in a rush, which creates massive erosion or deposition. What to do in this situation is a community affair and may require teamwork by a large group.

The longer we live in an area, the better we understand the natural cycles of our streams. It may take observations over more years than a lifetime to separate natural change from change caused by poor upstream management. We must look and learn and find a way to pass our knowledge on to land stewards of the future. If every generation learns from the successes and errors of the past, perhaps we will be gaining the wisdom and patience of nature.

Landscaping with Woody Plants

How we choose to landscape our home is a statement about our relation-
ship with the greater landscape around us. The Texas Hill Country is a land
of rugged conditions and beauty that is distinctly different from the tradi-
tional idea of a comfortable homesite. Nevertheless, drought, flood, sear-
ing heat, and killing frosts are part of the challenge. We live on a fragile
land that does not recover quickly, where our mistakes will be with us for a
very long time.

We need to know what is already here, appropriate, and useful. We
need to educate ourselves to see and understand the dynamics naturally
at work around us and then celebrate our unique and special place in the
world. There are many ways to learn to love and use the best of a native
landscape:

- Think local.
- Take your time.
- Know your soil. Although Hill Country soil is above a limestone
  base and consequently alkaline, there are important differences
  from place to place. Native plants have their own preferences.
- Look at the natural beauty all around, and choose what you want
  to include.
- Copy nature. Plants grow naturally in a mixture of many different
  species.
- Treasure the view, but keep your space connected to the ground.
- Avoid creating a sterile short-grass void under beautiful trees.
- Include vines in a natural landscape.
- Retain woody plants that are nurse plants for other, more vulner-
  able species.
- Save a grouping that will make a privacy screen or shelter a
  patio.
- Incorporate a thorny shrub that is a nurse plant for other natives
  that are vulnerable to deer browse.
- If you are building a house, blend your homesite landscape into
  the surrounding landscape.
- Pay attention to drainage, and plan for a natural look.

The Texas Hill Country has a special kind of beauty.

A rich diversity of native plant species is the basis of a healthy community.

- Know that a persistent drought will be interrupted by a major flood, and design a landscape to survive the worst conditions and thrive in the best.
- Accept the sun as the ruling design element in any Texas landscape.

Protection of the Landscape during Home and Other Construction

Save time and money by developing a landscape protection plan before construction begins. Careful planning will help avoid the expense and heartache of later repairing or removing trees located too close to construction activities.

Marking construction zone boundaries

Obtain a complete set of site development plans, including the proposed location of buildings, driveways, sidewalks, and utility lines. Ask the builder or architect to mark areas where heavy equipment will be used, where soil will be permanently added or removed and to what depth, and where fill and building materials will be temporarily stockpiled. Use a measuring tape, stakes, and string to temporarily mark the boundaries of construction activities.

Making an inventory of trees and shrubs

Record the location, size, and health of the plants in each area to be protected. Wilted leaves, broken or dead limbs, trunk rot, and thin tops are all signs of stress. In the area around the construction site, trees and shrubs that are overmature, lean heavily over the future building, or have severe insect or disease problems should be marked for removal prior to construction. Also, mark trees that need pruning to make room for future structures and construction equipment.

Selecting the areas to be saved

Examine the site carefully, and note how the native trees and shrubs fit into the landscape. Keep in mind that the builder may be able to shift the location of a building, utility line, or driveway. Follow these selection tips:

- Know your native woody plants, or get advice from someone who does.
- Consider all practical benefits of existing plants.
- Be sure you know exactly what you are removing.
- Maintain natural associations to provide wildlife with normal food and cover.
- Improve survival by saving groups instead of individuals.
- Be aware that large trees rarely survive within five feet of a new building.
- Retain a protection zone around individual trees with a radius in feet equal to the tree's diameter in inches measured at chest height.
- Transplant healthy young plants from within the construction zone.

Protect native plants during construction.

Protecting the areas you plan to save

Develop a map with the builder or architect that shows the location of areas to be protected and the safest route for access to the building zone. Then, install bright orange polypropylene fencing, and post "Off Limits" signs.

To protect delicate root systems, provide as much protected area as possible. Make sure all construction workers know that nothing inside this area is to be raked, cut, stored, or otherwise disturbed. Take several photographs of the areas to be protected before construction begins to document the protection methods used and the condition of the plants. A landscape protection contract signed by the builder and all contractors will help ensure compliance.

Preparing trees for construction disturbance
Take the following measures to protect trees prior to construction:
- Water regularly those special individuals that need their chances of survival enhanced when rainfall is less than normal.
- Fertilize those that are nutrient stressed. (For soil test information, contact your local County Cooperative Extension agent or Natural Resources Conservation Service office.)
- Prune branches that are dead, diseased, hazardous, or detrimental to the tree's natural form.

Monitoring the construction process
Visit the construction site regularly, and inspect the protected areas. Your presence alerts workers of your concern for the careful treatment of the trees and shrubs. Should damage occur, begin repairs as soon as possible. Immediately inform the builder of any violation in the landscape protection contract, and photograph the damage. Insist that all construction fences remain in place until all construction workers have left the site.

Making a final inspection of the construction site
After construction has been completed, evaluate the condition of the protected areas. Look for signs of damage or stress. It may take several years for severe problems to appear. Careful monitoring and preventive treatment such as watering may help minimize damage.

Simple Care for Native Trees and Shrubs
Although newly planted native trees and shrubs need to be watered about an inch each week during their first year, well-established native trees and shrubs do not usually require supplemental water, pruning, or fertilizer. In fact, overzealous care can kill a well-loved native tree or shrub. Nonetheless, to improve the appearance of particular native trees and shrubs, you may want to incorporate watering, pruning, fertilizing, and mulching of some individuals in your landscape-management plan.

Regular watering is not necessary for the survival of most native plants, even during a drought, although you may want to water some plants during water shortages to improve their appearance. During drought months, a simple rule of thumb can be followed to judge when and how much water will improve the health and appearance of most native trees and shrubs. Add the number of inches your area is short of the average monthly rainfall. Thus, if this month's average is two and a half inches and you measured only one inch, add about an inch and a half. Water established native trees and shrubs no more than once or twice a month, and water slowly and deeply, allowing the water to soak in and saturate the soil. Watering in the early morning will reduce excess evaporation and disease problems created by too much moisture over an extended period of time. Some trees, such as post oaks, are especially sensitive to excessive watering. Their leaves will turn yellow-green, and the tree may even die if the overwatering continues.

PRUNING

It is not necessary to prune dead or broken limbs from native trees and shrubs, but to improve the appearance of selected native trees and shrubs, you may want to do some pruning. If you do, follow these rules:
- Avoid cutting flush to the trunk or creating long stubs when pruning a limb.
- Clean the cutting tool with alcohol before pruning trees to prevent fungus or diseases.
- Paint all pruned ends on Spanish or live oak trees with any latex paint to avoid oak wilt infection.

FERTILIZER

It is best to fertilize native woody plants in early spring before leaves appear. Never fertilize native trees and shrubs during drought months. Avoid fertilizers that are high in nitrogen; use mild fertilizers with nitrogen-phosphorus-potassium proportions similar to 7-2-2 or 9-1-1.

MULCH

If you want to give special care to certain native trees and shrubs, add organic mulch over the ground within the canopy of their branches. For best results, mulch in early summer and early fall. Do not add mulch during the winter. Excess mulch will lower the soil temperature and may hold too much water in the ground, thus increasing incidence of fungal diseases. Also, when soil is wet and cold, essential nutrients are tied up in the soil and become unavailable to plants.

Oak Wilt

Oak wilt is caused by *Ceratocystis fagacearum,* a fungus that clogs a tree's water vessels. All oaks are susceptible, but it is a serious problem for live oaks and red oaks, including Spanish oak and blackjack oak. Spanish oaks die within seven to thirty days. Most live oaks die from three to twelve months after infection. There is, however, a natural 15–20 percent survival rate among live oaks.

Oak wilt spreads in two ways. Underground, it spreads from one tree to another through connected root systems that are especially common in live oaks. Underground infection results in patches of dead and dying live oak trees, expanding at an approximate rate of seventy-five feet per year. Aboveground, the fungus is carried by insects that pick up the spores from a fungal mat growing beneath the bark of an infected tree and take it to the wound of an uninfected tree, which becomes infected. Infection through insects occurs primarily in the spring.

IDENTIFICATION

In live oaks, a common symptom shows up on the leaves of infected limbs. The leaf veins will turn yellow-orange when the rest of the leaf is still green. The tips of some leaves may also turn brown. Once infected, most live oaks will gradually drop their leaves and die within a year. Some, however, survive in a reduced state with fewer leaves and a thin appearance.

In red oaks, such as Spanish oaks, the leaves first curl and wilt, then turn pale green and finally reddish brown, but they usually stay attached to the tree for some time. In these trees, fungal mats that are covered with spores may form under the bark. These mats make the tree very contagious. Fungal mats do not form in live oaks.

Live oak leaves show the symptoms of oak wilt.

PREVENTION

Never prune live oaks, Spanish oaks, or blackjack oaks from February through June. The safest times to prune are during the coldest days in mid-winter and the hot days of mid- to late summer. *Always* paint pruning cuts or natural wounds *immediately* (within 30 minutes) to prevent insects from being attracted to the wound.

Bulldozers used for clearing brush and trees nearly always hit and wound other trees. In areas where oak wilt is prevalent, clear only during January, July, August, September, or December, when the insects that spread the spores are inactive. Remove the contagious fungal mats by chipping, burning, or burying infected Spanish oaks soon after discovery.

Some observers have noticed that leaving cedar trees in the vicinity of live oaks slows the spread of oak wilt. This slower spread is probably due to a decreased number of live oak roots per unit of soil, so there are fewer connections between trees.

TREATMENT

There is no cure for oak wilt, but we can suppress the spread of the fungus through live oak roots and try to save live oaks that are in the line of infection. Sometimes, injecting a fungicide will save individual trees. This is not a cure because the fungus can still spread through the root systems. Treat high-value trees only within 75–150 feet of an infected tree. You can treat the trees yourself or hire a licensed pesticide applicator or, preferably, a trained arborist. When treating susceptible high-value trees, you should use a trained arborist with an applicator's license.

Trenches stop the underground spread of oak wilt by breaking the root connections between neighboring trees, but in order for this treatment to be effective, you must dig the trench deep enough to be below the lowest roots, usually four to five feet deep. Place the trench at least one hundred feet from the nearest symptomatic tree. In rural areas, when encircling a disease center, cut or uproot all trees within the barrier (except those injected with fungicide).

Before treating your trees for oak wilt, consult with a representative of the Texas Forest Service to learn about treatment based on the latest research.

LONG-TERM MANAGEMENT

Foster a diversity of tree species on your property by maintaining and planting an array of different, preferably native, trees that are well adapted to the Texas Hill Country. Plant resistant oak species or other native species, and avoid wounding susceptible oaks.

Naturalized, Invasive, Exotic Woody Plant Species

As early Europeans traveled from continent to continent, they introduced many plants to the new places they settled. Both European farming and ranching habits and the plants they introduced have had dramatic influences on these "new worlds."

Steer under pyracantha.

Some introduced plants, such as wheat and rice, are central to major agricultural industries that feed the human population. Others were unable to adapt to the new soil and climate and did not survive. Still others thrive and have become naturalized so that they are self-perpetuating in the wilds of their new homes. These we call *naturalized exotics*. Some naturalized exotics have been so successful that they are considered invasive, that is, they spread widely and often to the detriment of other plants. Not all invasive plants are exotic, but these are the ones considered here.

Of course, not all naturalized exotics came long ago with early European settlers. Many are plants that have been here for only a short time. An example is Chinese pistache, which was first introduced at Texas A&M University about thirty or forty years ago. Its female trees do not produce abundant seed until they are fifteen to twenty years old. Thus, there was a forty-year lag time before this species was recognized as a naturalized invasive. We walk a fine line in trying to incorporate plants that will enhance our gardens but hoping not to introduce plants that will spread rapidly through our native landscape, changing it beyond recognition. Many years may pass before we are able to identify an invasive plant with certainty.

Tree of heaven, *Ailanthus altissima.*

Texas Hill Country Invasive, Exotic Woody Plants

Nine woody and one grass exotic plant species that are naturalized and invasive in the Texas Hill Country are featured in this book. All are pictured, described, and discussed with the native species:

Chinese pistache, *Pistacia chinensis*
Heavenly bamboo, *Nandina domestica*
Japanese honeysuckle, *Lonicera japonica*
Chinese tallow, *Sapium sebiferum*
Chinaberry, *Melia azedarach*
Japanese privet, *Ligustrum japonicum*
Jujube, *Ziziphus zizyphus*
Firethorn, *Pyracantha koidzumii*
Chaste tree, *Vitex agnus-castus*
Giant reed, *Arundo donax*

Mimosa, *Albizia julibrissin.* Photo by Susan M. Sander

Black locust, *Robinia pseudoacacia*. Photo by Susan M. Sander

Golden rain tree, *Koelreuteria paniculata.*

Some other naturalized, invasive exotic species present in the Texas Hill
Country not described here include the following:

  Tree of heaven, *Ailanthus altissima*
  Mimosa, silk tree, *Albizia julibrissin*
  Black locust, *Robinia pseudoacacia*
  Golden rain tree, *Koelreuteria paniculata*
  Paper mulberry, *Broussonetia papyrifera*
  Chinese parasol tree, *Firmiana simplex*

Paper mulberry, *Broussonetia papyrifera*. Photo by Susan M. Sander

What do I do about invasive exotic species?

Current research to determine the most effective ways to remove problem exotic species has revealed that there is no simple answer. Certainly, it is best to prevent their spread by planting native species or, even better, only species native to your watershed; however, this is not always possible. Some invasive exotic species present such a serious impairment to native plant growth that the quality and essential character of large areas are changed. Physical removal, coupled with chemical treatment, may be necessary.

Japanese privet, or ligustrum, is difficult to remove by cutting alone because it often resprouts from the roots. The Texas Forest Service recommends cutting before the first frost and then painting the cut stump with concentrated Rodeo or Roundup. Keep cutting and treating until the root no longer resprouts.

The Nature Conservancy recommends that all Japanese honeysuckle on their land be killed by the following method: (1) treat from midautumn through early spring when it is easiest to spot and treat; (2) use foliar application of Roundup, Rodeo, or Accor applied after vegetation is dormant and when temperatures are above freezing or within two days of the first killing frost; (3) when possible, combine late fall or winter burn with herbicide treatment of resprouts about a month after they emerge. Further, the Nature Conservancy recommends avoiding soil disturbance in infested areas because it will enhance seed germination of the Japanese honeysuckle.

Are all invasive plants exotic?
By nature, pioneer plants, native or exotics, that thrive in disturbed sites are invasive. They move into newly changed places and, because they are well adapted to the situation, spread or invade the new habitat. These species are often unpopular because they change the landscape from the familiar to something new, which is often less productive both for wildlife and livestock.

A common pioneer plant scenario is Ashe juniper or poverty bush moving into an overgrazed and then abandoned hillside or pasture. The disturbance here was the removal of plants that the livestock preferred, as well as the action of their feet compacting and digging into the ground. The disturbance destroyed the former landscape, a thick mix of grasses and forbs, which will take many years to restore.

Fire is another form of disturbance, one that has occurred naturally for thousands of years. Our ecosystems can manage and adapt to fire. In fact, fire disturbance is necessary to maintain some prairie and marsh ecosystems. For this reason, controlled burns are a popular land-management tool. The heat of the fire kills many invasive trees and shrubs, releases nutrients into the soil, and stimulates dormant seed germination.

TREES, SHRUBS, AND VINES
OF THE TEXAS HILL COUNTRY

The trees, shrubs, and vines of the Texas Hill Country fall into three classes of vascular plants: Pinopsida, Magnoliopsida, and Liliopsida, which are presented here in phylogenetic order, or in their scientific place on the evolutionary scale. Within these classes, the plants are arranged alphabetically by family, and those in the same family, alphabetically by species.

In the plant descriptions, common names are listed first, followed by the scientific name and the name of the plant family in which the species occurs. The book *Vascular Plants of Texas* (1997) by Stanley D. Jones, Joseph K. Wipff, and Paul M. Montgomery served as the authority in matters of taxonomy and nomenclature.

Ten Texas Hill County invasive exotic species will be listed with the native plants in the same family.

CLASS: PINOPSIDA

Ashe Juniper, Cedar, Mountain Cedar
Juniperus ashei
Cupressaceae

Dominant evergreen shrub or small tree of the Texas Hill Country forming dense cedar brakes on limestone hillsides.

LEAVES: Tiny, scalelike, pressed into many little branches at ends of twigs; awl-shaped and sharp-pointed on seedlings and new growth.

FLOWERS: Minute male and female cones on separate plants; pollen produced by male trees, giving them a yellow cast and causing "cedar fever" allergies; winter.

FRUIT: Dark blue, juicy, berrylike cones, produced by female trees; summer–fall.

BARK: Gray, becomes shaggy with age and shreds into long, narrow, irregular strips; often colored by white or gray lichen patches.

RANGE: On limestone hills in Texas, Arkansas, Oklahoma, Missouri; south into Mexico and Guatemala.

Ashe juniper, commonly called "cedar," is an invasive plant and often forms dense, impenetrable thickets, or "cedar brakes," that provide good cover for deer and turkeys, especially in winter. It is an excellent natural windbreak or sound barrier as well as a fast-growing privacy fence, and it controls erosion on steep hillsides. The wood of Ashe juniper is resistant to decay and is still harvested extensively by cedar choppers for fence posts. A host plant to the olive hairstreak butterfly, its berries are eaten by many birds and mammals. In spring, bark from older trees growing in canyons and in association with Spanish oaks is used as nest material by the endemic and endangered golden-cheeked warbler.

Bill Ward

Bill Ward

Mexican Pinyon, Pinyon, Piñón, Pino Piñonero
Pinus cembroides (P. remota)
Pinaceae

Small to medium evergreen tree, growing in alkaline soil on dry, rocky slopes.

LEAVES: 2–3 needles per bundle but usually 2; blue to gray-green.

FLOWERS: Round, light brown or reddish cones at branch ends; mature in 2 years and shed seeds soon after.

FRUIT: Cones produce pine nuts with thin shells.

BARK: Red-brown to dark brown with shallow, irregular furrows and broad, scaly ridges.

RANGE: From 2,200–7,500 feet in Mexico, Arizona, and New Mexico. In Texas, on lower elevations of Trans-Pecos and Edwards Plateau, where its populations are distant from main distribution areas; on west-central Edwards Plateau near Camp Wood, Leakey, Rock Springs, and north of Bracketville.

At one time, the scattered populations of Mexican pinyon on the Edwards Plateau were considered a separate species, *P. remota*, and more recently a variety, *P. cembroides* var. *remota*. Whatever its classification, this is a lovely, heat- and drought-tolerant native pine appropriate for native plant gardening. It is available in a few native plant nurseries. Pine nuts are edible. On the Edwards Plateau they are a good food source for wildlife, including western scrub jays. Unfortunately, pine nut production is minimal during our many dry years.

Bald Cypress
Taxodium distichum
Taxodiaceae

A majestic deciduous, cone-bearing tree found lining permanent creeks and rivers throughout the Texas Hill Country.

LEAVES: Deciduous, alternate, feathery, ½–¾ inch long; pointed at tips, light green turning vivid rust in the fall.

FLOWERS: Male cones tan, 3–5 inches long in drooping clusters; female cones spherical, single or in groups; March–April.

FRUIT: Wrinkled, green spheres, 1 inch in diameter; spheres ripen and turn brown October–December.

BARK: Thin, fairly smooth, gray or tan with long, shallow ridges.

WOOD: Straight-grained; not strong but very durable and resistant to decay.

RANGE: In swamps and along permanent streams from Central Texas east to Florida and NORTH TO Delaware and Illinois.

Bald cypress grew when dinosaurs dominated extensive Texas swamps. Eons later, Kerrville was founded as a mill town in 1852 when bald cypress trees were being lumbered extensively from Hill Country rivers and creeks. Old homes and barns in this area often are made of extremely wide cypress boards. This wood also was used extensively for shingles, siding, flooring, buckets, railroad ties, and bridge timbers.

Because the bald cypress's thick, stiff limbs grow at right angles to the trunk, they often break in strong winds. Old creek beds or riverbeds can be identified by the presence of cypress trees because their seeds can sprout only in extremely wet conditions found along a permanent stream. The cones are food for many kinds of wildlife, and cavity nesters such as wood ducks use old, hollow cypress trees. A bald cypress tree can be grown as an ornamental if it receives adequate water. Its fast growth rate, graceful shape, and bright fall color make it a beautiful landscape tree.

CLASS:
MAGNOLIOPSIDA

**Bigtooth Maple, Plateau
Bigtooth Maple,
Uvalde Bigtooth Maple**
Acer grandidentatum **var.**
sinuosum
Aceraceae
A small tree with a rounded crown
and slender trunk that grows in pro-
tected canyons along some creeks of
Real, Uvalde, Bandera, and Kendall
counties.

LEAVES: Deciduous, opposite, simple,
2–3 ½ inches long and wide,
3-lobed, with smooth margins.

FLOWERS: In short, stalked clusters
with only a few yellow blooms;
appear with the leaves in early
spring.

FRUIT: Attached in pairs, each with
a long, down-curved tan wing;
appears in summer and ripens in
fall.

BARK: Thin and gray, becoming dark
brown with age and developing
platelike scales.

RANGE: In some of the deeper, well-
watered canyons from Boerne in
Kendall County west to the Lost
Maples State Park of Real County;
in the north-south dry canyons
of the Lampasas Cut Plains; and
in sheltered, usually dry, canyons within the mountains of the
Trans-Pecos.

This tree is the namesake of the Lost
Maples State Park near Leakey, Texas.
Once abundant during an earlier
time when a cooler, wetter climate
existed in the area, this species now is
restricted to isolated, protected locations. Trees are most easily spotted
in dense growth along rocky stream
banks in November when they turn
into a blaze of yellow, orange, and/
or red.

Box Elder, Ashleaf Maple
Acer negundo
Aceraceae

A fast-growing understory species that is our most common and most unpopular maple.

LEAVES: Deciduous, 6–15 inches long, pinnately compound, 3–9 leaflets, often only 3; edges toothed or with shallow lobes.

FLOWERS: Small, greenish, no petals, on slender stalks; pollinated by wind and bees; March–May.

FRUIT: Typical paired maple wings that hang in clusters; ripens September–October.

BARK: Green, smooth, and thin on seedlings; later, gray–brown with rounded ridges and shallow fissures.

RANGE: Most widespread of any maple species, from the East Coast to California and from Canada to Mexico and Guatemala; through human intervention, naturalized far outside its natural range, for example, into the Pacific Northwest and New Mexico.

Box elder spreads rapidly, and its bad habits keep it out of favor: ragged growth pattern, short life span, many sprouts from the trunk, prolific seedlings, a shallow root system, and a tendency to be easily damaged by wind, insects, and fungus. Seedlings are often found near streams far from the parent tree. But its seeds are popular with birds and squirrels. Its "leaves of three" can be confused with those of poison ivy; but box elder leaves are opposite, and poison ivy leaves are alternate.

American Smoke Tree
Cotinus obovatus
Anacardiaceae

Unique, uncommon shrub or small tree found on the highest bluffs and hills in Kendall, Kerr, and Bandera counties.

LEAVES: Deciduous, simple, oval, waxy, alternate, mostly in a clump at the end of small branches; smooth olive-green above, paler and fuzzy below; edges smooth and sometimes wavy, veins obvious above; petioles or leaf stems purple or reddish.

FLOWERS: Male and female flowers usually on separate trees; large, open, feathery clusters with a few greenish yellow blossoms; flower stems turn purple; April–May.

FRUIT: Very small, light brown, on slender, hairy stalks; late May.

BARK: Dark gray–black, rough, broken into small, thin scales.

RANGE: Rare in mountains of Alabama, Tennessee, and Missouri; west to Oklahoma and Central Texas.

The American smoke tree is easily overlooked because it is often a half-hidden understory shrub or a small, old, gnarled tree in a high, rough place. A reliable distinguishing characteristic is its oval leaves that grow on red leaf stems and mostly in clumps at the end of small branches. It is most easily spotted in the spring by the smoky appearance of blossoms gone to seed (see p. 7) or in the fall by its bright foliage. The wood is highly resistant to rotting and produces a yellow dye that was used extensively during the 1860s. An unusual and attractive ornamental, this tree keeps a more regular shape in cultivation. There it can be mistaken for another species in this genus, the European smoke tree (*C. coggygria*), that is widely planted in the eastern United States.

INVASIVE EXOTIC SPECIES

Chinese Pistache
Pistacia chinensis
Anacardiaceae
Native to central China; newly invasive, exotic species.

LEAVES: Pinnately compound, 10 or more leaflets 2–4 inches long, may or may not have a terminal leaflet.

FLOWERS: Male and female flowers on different trees; loose clusters, green, no petals; April.

FRUIT: Only on female trees, small, red, in loose clusters; turns dark blue as it ripens in fall.

BARK: On young plants, light brown with lighter splotches, then with flat ridges and wide lighter brown fissures; later, fissures narrow, ridges often break off into shaggy flakes; on mature trees, dark gray or gray-brown with odd-shaped scales.

RANGE: From China; beginning to escape cultivation and spread into the wild around urban areas in Central Texas.

Chinese pistache is an attractive, deciduous tree with long, pinnately compound leaves, turning bright yellow and red in the fall. Texas A&M University was one of the first locations for the introduction of this Chinese species thirty to forty years ago. Its seeds are spread by birds, and the original trees have produced reproductive offspring growing wild in several locations.

Aromatic Sumac, Skunkbush
Rhus aromatica
Anacardiaceae

Medium-sized, attractive, aromatic shrub frequent in fencerows and thickets, with distinct three-part leaves.

LEAVES: Deciduous, alternate, compound, with 3 leaflets, each wider and lobed at tip end; pungent when crushed.

FLOWERS: Buds in winter look like small, soft, red spikes; open before leaves appear; small, yellow, numerous, on eye-catching spikes at branch ends; March–April.

FRUIT: Small, fleshy, red, covered with fuzz; ripens in June.

RANGE: From California east to Central Texas and from Mexico to North Texas.

The smallest of the Hill Country sumac species, aromatic sumac often is overlooked, but its interesting scent, conspicuous spring blossoms, and beautiful red fall color make it a desirable and attractive shrub. The fruit is eaten by many songbirds and game birds. Slender twigs are used to produce a yellow dye and are mixed with willow in Native American basket weaving.

Flameleaf Sumac, Prairie Flameleaf Sumac, Shumac
Rhus lanceolata
Anacardiaceae

An open, branching shrub or small tree with slender branches; common on dry rocky hillsides, old fields, and fencerows and openings in cedar-oak woodlands.

LEAVES: Deciduous, alternate, compound; 9–21 paired leaflets with 1 on tip end, leaflets shiny and smooth on upper surface; turn brilliant red in fall.

FLOWERS: Small, creamy white, in clusters up to 5 inches long on ends of branches; summer.

FRUIT: Forms distinct dense clusters at branch ends, red when ripe; turns brown after leaves have fallen, persists through winter.

BARK: Gray or brown, usually smooth but with small scales on older trees.

RANGE: From Oklahoma south to eastern Mexico and from New Mexico east to Central Texas.

The leaflets of flameleaf sumac contain tannin and have been used to replace oak bark in tanning leather. The seeds can be crushed to make a refreshing lemon-flavored drink. Dependable scarlet fall color makes flameleaf sumac a good ornamental, especially along fences, because it spreads by root suckers that form loose thickets. Its fruit is an especially important food source for quail, grouse, and other birds.

Desert Sumac, Littleleaf Sumac
Rhus microphylla
Anacardiaceae
Round, deciduous shrub or, rarely, a
short tree, with many branches.
LEAVES: Small, pinnately compound;
with narrow wings growing on
either side of the center line; 5–9
leaflets covered with long, fine
hairs.
FLOWERS: Tiny, white, crowded into
small clusters; April.
FRUIT: Small, round, red-orange, in a
tight bunch, also with fine hairs.

Desert sumac grows on the dry western parts of the Edwards Plateau and
is also a minor component of South
Texas brushland. Its flowers attract
flies, and it grows in dry, rugged land

mixed with other brush. Desert sumac is a good wildlife plant: its dense
structure provides cover for birds,
small mammals, and lizards and good
nest sites for breeding birds. Deer will
browse leaves and twigs. Its fruit is
eaten by small mammals and birds,
including quail and turkeys. When
crushed and mixed with water and
sugar, desert sumac fruit can also be
made into "sumac-ade" for humans.
Native plant gardeners use this plant
as a drought-tolerant landscape
shrub.

Evergreen Sumac
Rhus virens
Anacardiaceae

A large shrub found in gullies and along country roads on rocky slopes, commonly growing in a sculpted, round shape.

LEAVES: Evergreen, alternate, compound; 5–9 leaflets in pairs with 1 at tip end, leaflets leathery, dark green, shiny on upper surface and dull on lower surface; turn dull orange, yellow, or brown in fall.

FLOWERS: Tiny, creamy white blossoms; appear in small clusters among the leaves during summer with adequate rain.

FRUIT: In clusters, small, flattened, covered with red hairs; ripens in early fall.

RANGE: Central and West Texas, New Mexico, and Mexico.

This is the only evergreen sumac in the Texas Hill Country and is available in some native plant nurseries. The Comanche called it "Tamaichia" and collected and sun-dried fall leaves to mix with tobacco for smoking. The leaves also have been used locally to treat asthma symptoms. The fruit quenches thirst when held on the tongue. Evergreen sumac is a host plant to the dusky-blue groundstreak butterfly. Flowers provide excellent late summer forage for bees and butterflies. The attractive red fruit is important food for birds and small mammals and usually remains until Christmas.

Poison Ivy
Toxicodendron radicans
Anacardiaceae

A shrub or vigorous climbing vine, often abundant at woodland edges and easily identified by its shiny, green "leaflets of three."

LEAVES: Compound, each with 3 leaflets that vary in size but usually have large, obvious, lobed teeth; shiny, green above.

FLOWERS: Greenish, white, inconspicuous, in clusters, fragrant; summer.

FRUIT: Small, dirty white, round, in loose clumps; fall, and persist on bare twigs in winter.

RANGE: All across United States; Canada, Mexico, and West Indies.

Poison ivy climbs by tiny roots that stick to tree bark, posts, and so on. Near a stream, an old vine will grow to great heights on a tree, tightly attached to its tree by thick masses of these rootlets. *T. radicans* has several varieties in the Hill Country that are similar. All contain toxicodendrol, the poisonous oil that produces blisters and itching in many individuals. This oil is in all parts of the plant, but it takes about twenty minutes to penetrate the skin and can be rinsed off during this time to prevent ill effects. Poison ivy is good for wildlife. Deer like its leaves, and many birds eat its berries. Poison ivy is a host plant to the dusky-blue groundstreak butterfly.

Possumhaw, Deciduous Holly
Ilex decidua
Aquifoliaceae

Common large bush or small tree in fencerows and thickets and near water.

LEAVES: Simple, deciduous, alternate, or several together on very short branches, 1 ½–3 inches long; generally round at tip end and tapered at base; edges with round teeth, each having a gland visible with a 10x hand lens.

FLOWERS: Small, white, appear with new leaves; March–May.

FRUIT: Small, round, bright red-or-ange, solitary or 2–3 together, only on female plants; fall, and persists through the winter.

BARK: Smooth, thin, mottled gray, sometimes with wartlike bumps.

RANGE: Texas east to Florida and north to Kansas and Indiana.

Possumhaw is in the holly family. Female plants, which have bright red-orange berries that often last all winter, are popular landscape plants. Male plants do not have berries and are rather nondescript. Female plants are available in local nurseries under the name deciduous yaupon. Possumhaw berries are eaten by birds and small mammals, usually in late winter. It is a host plant to the dusky-blue groundstreak butterfly.

Yaupon Holly, Yaupon
Ilex vomitoria
Aquifoliaceae

Very popular and widely distributed
landscape shrub or small tree with
bright red berries, single- or multi-
trunked, found in wooded canyons
and bottomlands.

LEAVES: Simple, alternate, evergreen,
   upper surface shiny, with small
   rounded teeth, tip has gland visible with 10x hand lens, ½ to 2
   inches long, half as wide.

FLOWERS: Small, white, male and
   female flowers on separate plants;
   April and May.

FRUIT: Bright red, fleshy, ¼-inch
   diameter, poisonous; fall and
   winter.

BARK: Light gray-brown to mottled
   dark gray, smooth and tight, with
   small scales on old trunks.

RANGE: From Central Texas as far
   west as the Frio River, north to
   Oklahoma and Arkansas, east to
   Virginia and Florida.

Yaupon holly is native east and
southeast of the Hill Country. Like all
holly berries, native yaupon berries
are poisonous and can cause vomiting and diarrhea. At one time Native
Americans living in East Texas used
Ilex vomitoria to make "Black Drink,"
which they drank in an annual cer-
emony. This was described at length
in a report written in 1542 by early
Spanish explorer Cabeza de Vaca.

Yaupon holly is still popular today,
but now as a lovely ornamental landscape plant. Landscapers familiar with
native plants recommend grouping
it with Carolina buckthorn, Mexican
buckeye, possumhaw, and spicebush
to create natural understory in an
attractive woodland garden. Yaupon
holly is slow growing but widely
adaptable and will grow in sun or
shade, as well as different soil types.
It is tolerant of poor drainage and
drought.

Bearded Swallow-wort, Thicket Threadvine
Cynanchum barbigerum
Asclepiadaceae

Small twining vine on low plants, shrubs, and other vines that stays less than 6 feet high and is hard to spot unless you look closely.

LEAVES: Up to 2 inches long, slender, lance-shaped.

FLOWERS: Tiny, ⅛ inch wide, cream-colored, in small clusters; May–August.

RANGE: Edwards Plateau, South Texas brushland, coastal plains, and the Trans-Pecos.

Bearded swallow-wort is a host plant for the variegated fritillary butterfly. When you find this vine, look for the fritillary's caterpillar, which is orange with rows of black spines along its body. Its pupa is tan with some red, white, and black spots. Bearded swallow-wort is nutritious browse for deer, but its small size limits its impact.

Pearl Milkweed, Green Milkweed Vine, Net-vein Milkvine
Matelea reticulata
Asclepiadaceae

A twining vine with slender stems growing in open woodlands, along fencerows, and in thickets, sometimes climbing 12 feet into small trees.

LEAVES: Opposite, large, heart-shaped, 2–4 inches long; covered with soft, spreading hairs.

FLOWERS: Pale green, stiff, flat; 5 petals covered with netlike veins, joining to make a star shape and with a small pearly dot in the center of the star; summer–fall.

FRUIT: Slender, green, spiny pod, 2–4 inches long; turns maroon when seeds are mature.

RANGE: Central, South, and West Texas.

There is another uncommon and similar climbing milkweed vine in the Texas Hill Country: plateau milkweed vine (*M. edwardensis*), which is endemic to the Edwards Plateau. *M. edwardensis* is distinguished by its bell-shaped flowers that lack a central "pearly" dot.

Pearl milkweed, as well as other milkweed plants, is a host plant to the monarch butterfly. All members of the milkweed family show a milky white sap when a stem is broken. This fluid contains an alkaloid that renders the monarch caterpillar and butterfly poisonous to birds, thus protecting them from predation.

Wavy Leaf Milkweed Vine, Wavy Leaf Twinevine
Sarcostemma crispum (Funastrum crispum)
Asclepiadaceae

Small, easily overlooked vine up to 6 feet long that commonly grows in limestone and granite soil on fences and other vines.

LEAVES: In pairs along the stem, up to 4 inches long, narrow, lance-shaped, edges wavy.

FLOWERS: Dark rust red, about ½ inch wide; April–June, and later with rain.

FRUIT: Long milkweed pod with pointed end, first green and then tan; seems oversized for such a small vine.

RANGE: Central and South Texas west to California.

Wavy leaf milkweed vine is a host plant to queen, soldier, and monarch butterflies. It is a good example of how an unremarkable plant can be important to other creatures and thus important to the healthy balance of an ecosystem.

Another species, climbing milkweed vine (*S. cynanchoides*), is found trailing along the ground or climbing over bushes on sandy soil. It has thick clusters of greenish white flowers, some with pale purple or pink markings, and arrowhead-shaped leaves 1–2 inches long.

Poverty Bush, Roosevelt Weed, False Willow
Baccharis neglecta
Asteraceae

Loose, airy bush extremely common in fallow fields, on roadsides, and in other disturbed places.

LEAVES: Partly evergreen, simple, alternate, very narrow, up to 3 inches long.

FLOWERS: Male and female flowers on separate plants; silvery white female flowers in loose plumes; October–November.

FRUIT: Tiny, carried by the wind; fall-winter.

RANGE: Southern plant from North Carolina west to Arizona.

Because of very narrow, light green leaves, poverty bush is sometimes mistaken for young willow. The female plant's silvery white plumes are especially beautiful in the late afternoon sun. Poverty bush is often used by resting monarch butterflies during their fall migration. It is good for erosion control in dry, disturbed places. Poverty bush is an invasive pioneer plant in disturbed places, and its extensive root system prevents erosion.

Damianita
Chrysactinia mexicana
Asteraceae

Low, 16 inches tall or less, mounding, rugged, evergreen shrub; locally common in overgrazed pastures on southern edge of Texas Hill Country.

LEAVES: Very small, narrow, less than ½ inch long, crowded on stems; aromatic when crushed.

FLOWERS: Tiny, bright yellow, daisylike, on slender stems up to 3 inches long; April–May, and later in summer and early fall with significant rain.

FRUIT: Very small and inconspicuous.

RANGE: From south-central Texas south and west, New Mexico, and northern Mexico.

fact, the quickest way to kill it is with water in poorly drained soil. Without its beautiful flowers, damianita is, at best, nondescript.

Damianita is a beautiful wildflower and can be a very good landscape plant. It is drought tolerant and will grow under the worst conditions. In

Texas Barberry
Berberis swaseyi
Berberidaceae

Uncommon shrub that looks very much like agarita; found only in the Texas Hill Country.

LEAVES: Persistent, compound, with 5–9 leaflets, each with 7–13 pointed teeth; edges may be dark red under stress; turn deep red or purple in fall.

FLOWERS: Yellow, nearly ½ inch wide, fragrant, in clusters; March–April.

FRUIT: Yellow-white to reddish berry, ¼–½ inch wide, edible.

RANGE: Endemic to Texas Hill Country; frequent in areas of Hayes and Comal counties; a few in Kerr, Bandera, and Real counties.

Texas barberry can be locally common, as in Wimberley. It was first found along the Pedernales River. Texas barberry is a low shrub and a good source of food for resident and migrant birds. Butterflies flock to nectar at its blossoms. Whenever you find this endemic species, monitor and protect it as needed. It can be grown as an ornamental and is resistant to cold and drought.

Agarita, Agarito
Berberis trifoliata
Berberidaceae

Very common across the Texas Hill Country, where it can be found on dry, rocky ground and in pastures and thickets.

LEAVES: Evergreen, compound, 3 skinny leaflets, with 5 sharp points; can be dark green but usually covered with a gray-blue tinge.

FLOWERS: Yellow, small, fragrant, in clusters; February–April.

FRUIT: Abundant, bright red berries; ripen in June.

RANGE: Central, West, and North Texas; New Mexico, Arizona, and Mexico.

Because deer and livestock avoid its sharp leaves, a stout agarita bush will provide excellent protective cover for birds and small mammals that also eat the plentiful berries. The berries make good jelly, but because of the heavily armored leaves, you must use a stick to beat the berries off the bush and onto a sheet to avoid lacerations from the thorns. Agarita wood is bright yellow and can be used to make a tan-orange dye. The roots contain an alkaloid that is toxic to bacteria and protozoans and has been used medicinally to treat toothache and stomach trouble. Agarita flowers are an important bee forage.

INVASIVE EXOTIC SPECIES

Nandina, Heavenly Bamboo
Nandina domestica
Berberidaceae
Very common, exotic, evergreen, ornamental shrub in southern United States and Japan.
LEAVES: Lance-shaped, 2–3 pinnately compound, much longer than wide, smooth; often green with red.
FLOWERS: Cream-colored, on long, branched inflorescence.

FRUIT: Small, round, red.
RANGE: India to eastern Asia.

Nandina is a popular garden plant that has escaped into the wild, especially into sandy woods. Its leaves produce cyanogenic compounds.

Trumpet Creeper
Campsis radicans
Bignoniaceae

An attractive vine with large, orange, tube-shaped blossoms; found climbing fences, shrubs, and trees in good soil.

LEAVES: Opposite, up to 12 inches long, pinnately compound, 5–11 leaflets; dark green above and lighter below; oval with an elongated tip with coarse, saw-toothed margins.

FLOWERS: Showy, red-orange, tubular blossoms; 2–3 ½ inches long, with 5 lobes in flat clusters at branch ends; May–October.

FRUIT: Rounded pods, 2–6 inches long; narrow on either end, with 2 lengthwise ridges; split open when mature revealing numerous thin-winged, brown seeds.

RANGE: Central Texas east to Florida and north to New Jersey and Iowa.

Anne Adams

Trumpet creeper is a popular landscape vine that can be found in local nurseries. In the wild, this woody vine is more common in East Texas where there is better soil and more rain than in the Hill Country. In Central Texas, trumpet creeper is most often found in river valleys or near old buildings where it has escaped cultivation. Its blossoms attract hummingbirds.

Desert Willow, Mimbre
Chilopsis linearis
Bignoniaceae

Loose, often leaning, small tree with gorgeous, lavender-pink, trumpet-shaped flowers and willow-like leaves, found along streams and dry beds on western edge of Texas Hill Country.

LEAVES: Opposite or alternate, very narrow, pointed, usually about 4 inches long but can range from 3–10 inches, sometimes sticky.

FLOWERS: Showy, tubular, usually pink or lavender but may be white or dark rose, 1–3 inches long; May–September.

FRUIT: In slender, woody pod 5–8 inches long, seeds are numerous, flat, oval, winged with hairy tufts.

BARK: Smooth when young, changing to broad ridges with deep narrow fissures on old trees.

RANGE: From the western edge of the Texas Hill Country west to California and south deep into northern Mexico.

Desert willow is a lovely, West Texas tree that is programmed to burst into bloom after a heavy rain. A popular fast-growing and drought-tolerant landscape tree, desert willow needs well-drained soil and full sun and grows naturally along dry streams that are subject to flooding and disturbance. Its roots help stabilize new soil and are important in erosion control.

Some Native Americans of the southwest used its branches to make bows, and in Mexico "Mimbre" branches are used to weave baskets. The flowers are pollinated by insects, and purple stripes or "bee guides" on the blossoms help direct bees to the nectar within. Its flowers grow on new wood, and it can be pruned to encourage more blossoms.

Emilie Rogers

Anaqua, Anacua, Sandpaper Tree
Ehretia anacua
Boraginaceae

Where it grows naturally in the Texas Hill Country, a large shrub or multi-trunked tree of protected river valleys and canyons.

LEAVES: Simple, dark green, 1 ½–3 inches long; heavy sandpaper texture, edges smooth or with slight teeth; usually evergreen.

FLOWERS: White, less than ½ inch wide, star-shaped, fragrant, in clusters at the ends of small branches; April.

FRUIT: Round, about ¼ inch wide; first green, then yellow-orange; fleshy, edible.

RANGE: South-central Texas into northern Mexico; grows along the Colorado River in Austin, where it is at the northern edge of its range.

Anaqua is a South Texas brushland tree that at one time was a popular ornamental planting in cities, towns, and farmyards. It grows slowly and has a distinctive, solid character. You cannot miss its dark foliage and sandpaper leaves. Anaqua growing in the Hill Country will need protection from the cold north wind to avoid freeze damage.

The genus name *Ehretia* honors an artist, George Dionysius Ehret, who illustrated plants in the 1700s. The species name is a variation of its local Native American name. In New Braunfels, the anaqua is called *Vogel-beerenbaum*, which means "birdberry tree." Birds and mammals love the small but sweet anaqua fruit. The tree's dense foliage produces good wildlife shelter, and bees nectar heavily on the April blossoms. The leaves are shed and replaced in early spring.

**Tasajillo, Pencil Cactus,
Desert Christmas Cactus**
Opuntia leptocaulis
Cactaceae
Shrublike cactus that grows singly or
in dense thickets, in bottomland soil,
on fencerows, and under trees.
STEMS: Pencil-stemmed, jointed
    and easily detached; sections
    6–8 inches long, with spines 1–2
    inches long.
FLOWERS: Inconspicuous, small,
    yellow-green or bronze, appear on
    stems; open only late in evening;
    May–August.

FRUIT: Many small, bright red, juicy
    berries.
RANGE: Southwestern Oklahoma,
    Texas, New Mexico, Arizona, and
    Mexico.

Tasajillo grows to about 5 feet tall
and has many crowded branches.
Beware of direct encounters because
stems of the plant detach and "at-
tack" the offender. On the other
hand, tasajillo is a good wildlife
plant, containing 8 percent protein
throughout the year. Birds, including
quail and turkeys, and deer and small
mammals eat the fruit.

White Honeysuckle
Lonicera albiflora
Caprifoliaceae

An attractive climbing shrub with branches that twine around and through adjacent trees and bushes.

LEAVES: Simple, broad, oval, round at tip with tiny point, smooth and fairly stiff; uppermost leaves attached at their base to form a collar around the blossom cluster and, later in the year, around clusters of red berrylike fruit.

FLOWERS: White or yellow-white, in clusters at ends of stems; spring.

FRUIT: Bright, translucent red clusters that stand out as the leaves drop off; October–November.

RANGE: Central and West Texas north to Oklahoma and west to New Mexico and Arizona; also in Mexico.

White honeysuckle blossoms strongly resemble those of the extremely common, invasive Japanese honeysuckle from eastern Asia. The native white honeysuckle is noninvasive. Its attractive spring blossoms and bright red berries make it a good landscape plant, which is available at some local growers and nurseries. The fruit, favored by birds and small mammals, was at one time used medicinally as a laxative and to induce vomiting.

INVASIVE EXOTIC SPECIES

Japanese Honeysuckle
Lonicera japonica
Caprifoliaceae

Evergreen, twining vine that forms extensive, thick masses over fences and shrubs.

LEAVES: Simple, variable shape, ¾–1 ½ inches long; with smooth margins; various shades of green; upper leaves not attached to form a collar around the blossoms.

FLOWERS: Fragrant, white to yellow petals form tube greater than ½ inch long; April–May.

FRUIT: Black, ¼–½ inch wide; September–November.

RANGE: From eastern Asia, including Japan and Korea; naturalized throughout United States except for northern states from Minnesota to Washington.

Japanese honeysuckle spreads by seeds, underground stems, and aboveground runners and invades disturbed places, floodplains, and forest edges. It is able to outcompete native vegetation for light and soil nutrients because of its rapid growth rate, wide seed dispersal, lack of natural enemies, and extended growing season. The presence of Japanese honeysuckle has been proven to suppress the growth of native trees and shrubs.

The Nature Conservancy recommends that property be surveyed regularly and all Japanese honeysuckle plants destroyed immediately. For more information on control of this invasive species, see the separate section on invasive alien species.

Coral Honeysuckle
Lonicera sempervirens
Caprifoliaceae

Evergreen twining vine with gorgeous red, tube-shaped flowers that grows in the eastern half of the Texas Hill Country.

LEAVES: Simple, oval, in pairs, smooth, fairly stiff; leaves nearest the flowers attached at their base to form a collar around the blossoms.

FLOWERS: Brilliant red or orange blossoms in shape of slender tube, up to 2 inches long, in clusters at ends of shoots; spring–fall with adequate rain.

FRUIT: Red-orange, about ¼ inch wide.

RANGE: From Texas to Florida and north to Connecticut and Nebraska.

Coral honeysuckle is a native component of Texas Hill Country brush, growing over fairly deep soil and in sunny locations where the soil surface and plant roots are insulated from the heat of the sun. It is a popular landscape plant because of its showy blooms and noninvasive growth. Coral honeysuckle is drought tolerant and, once established, will need no more than three to six soakings per year.

Common Elderberry
Sambucus canadensis
Caprifoliaceae

Tall, partly woody shrub with many stems growing from the base that is found on permanent streams and rivers and in low, wet places.

LEAVES: Large, up to 12 inches long, deciduous, opposite, compound; 4–10 paired leaflets and 1 at tip end; leaflets 2–5 inches long, oval with pointed tips, and teeth on the margins.

FLOWERS: Many small blossoms, white, 5-petaled, in large flat flower heads; May–July.

FRUIT: Edible, juicy, dark purple when ripe, each with 3–4 small yellow seeds; often present when flowers still blooming.

RANGE: From Texas north to Manitoba and east to Florida and Nova Scotia.

This popular plant has had numerous practical uses for many years. Ripe elderberries are high in vitamin C and make good wine, pies, and jellies. They also have been used to treat cough and sore throat caused by the common cold. The flowers can be dipped in batter and fried as fritters. Native Americans soaked them in water to make a refreshing summer drink. Dried leaves have been used as an insecticide and as a poultice for sores, tumors, and sore joints. The bark makes a black dye. The stems, with pith removed, were once used to tap maple trees, make whistles, flutes, and popguns. Elderberry is an important wildlife food. The foliage is sometimes browsed by deer, and its berries are eaten by forty-five different species of birds.

Rusty Blackhaw, Cramp Bark Tree
Viburnum rufidulum
Caprifoliaceae

Small understory tree or large bush found in thickets and individually along fencerows and streams in canyons and open woodlands.

LEAVES: Simple, opposite, glossy green, usually deciduous in late fall; oval, 1–3 inches long; edges with small teeth, and tip end pointed or slightly indented; fine rust red hairs covering winter buds, leaf stems, and center vein on lower leaf surface.

FLOWERS: Small, creamy white; in large, round, but flattened clusters; after the leaves appear in March and April.

FRUIT: Edible, small, dark blue, football-shaped; ripens in early fall and quickly eaten by birds and other animals.

RANGE: From Virginia and Florida west to southern Illinois, Missouri, Oklahoma, and Texas.

Rusty blackhaw is easily recognized in spring by eye-catching white blossoms and in late fall by shiny, maroon leaves. It can be a good landscape shrub because it is versatile and tough and has showy spring blossoms, shiny leaves, and outstanding fall color. The fruit tastes like raisins and can be eaten raw or cooked if you find it before wildlife does. Pioneers used the fruit in jellies, stews, and sauces. At one time, the root bark was used to make a drug used to relieve menstrual cramps.

Texas Bindweed
Convolvulus equitans
Convolvulaceae
Common, twining vine that grows
to about 6 feet long on fences, small
shrubs, and other low plants.
LEAVES: Variable, 1–3 inches long,
   with overall arrow shape.
FLOWERS: Funnel-shaped, about
   1 inch wide, white with bright
   pink-red center; April–October.
FRUIT: Round, tan, less than ½ inch
   wide.
RANGE: Texas, Arkansas, Oklahoma,
   Kansas, New Mexico, Colorado,
   Utah, Arizona, and California.

Texas bindweed is an ingredient of
the tangled shrubbery that naturally
grows all over the Texas Hill Country. It is found in places where vines,
shrubs, and small trees grow together
in a mix that creates food and shelter
for small birds, lizards, and mammals. Covered with tiny, gray hairs,
Texas bindweed does not grow in
huge, expansive clumps as Alamo
vine does, but the bright white and
red flowers and unusual leaves make
it easy to spot and identify.

Wild Morning Glory, Tievine
Ipomoea cordatotriloba
(Ipomoea trichocarpa)
Convolvulaceae

Very common, low twining vine throughout the Texas Hill Country; especially easy to see in the summer when its lavender flowers may be the only blossom in sight.

LEAVES: About 2 inches long, heart-shaped or with deep lobes, surfaces smooth.

FLOWERS: Funnel-shaped, about 2 inches wide, pink-lavender with darker purple center; April–October.

RANGE: Texas, Mexico, and southeastern United States.

Wild morning glory is the Hill Country's most common morning glory. It is often considered a weed because it has the habit of moving into disturbed areas, such as gardens. On the other hand, wild morning glory is a tough plant that can tolerate the summer heat and blossom when everything else has finished blooming. It is a host plant to the variegated fritillary butterfly.

Locally, wild morning glory is called bindweed, but this name is officially restricted to the genus *Convolvulus* in an attempt to eliminate confusion between these two genera. The local *Convolvulus* species is *C. equitans,* commonly called Texas bindweed.

Lindheimer's Morning Glory
Ipomoea lindheimeri
Convolvulaceae
An infrequent and isolated vine with
distinctive lobed leaves and huge,
delicate morning glory blossoms that
twines through thickets, climbs on
dry fencerows, and spreads across
grassy places.
LEAVES: With 3–7 deep lobes constricted toward the center and
pointed at the tips, 1–3 ½ inches
long; both surfaces covered with
short, straight hairs.
FLOWERS: Pale blue or lavender with
white center, about 3 inches long
and 2 inches wide; open in morning and close with the heat of the
day; April–October.

FRUIT: Seeds in round, 4-chambered,
½-inch capsule; covered with
5 fuzzy sepals 1 ¼ inches long;
produced with the blossoms;
April–October.
RANGE: Endemic to Edwards Plateau
west to the Trans-Pecos.

Lindheimer's morning glory is a
hardy perennial vine named for early
Texas botanist Ferdinand Lindheimer,
who made a living collecting new
Texas specimens for museums in the
East. He settled in New Braunfels,
and this plant can be found growing
in the backyard of his home, which is
now a small historical museum.

Alamo Vine, Correhuela de las Doce
Merremia dissecta (Ipomoea dissecta)
Convolvulaceae

Grows in extensive masses with many blossoms on disturbed soil, on fence-rows, near streams, and in dry fields.

LEAVES: With 5–7 lobes having a common center, each lobe with deep, wavy edges; 1 ½–2 ½ inches long.

FLOWERS: White with pink-red center, about 2 inches wide; May–October.

RANGE: Central and South Texas; not native to Florida but has spread from cultivated plantings into the wild in that state.

Alamo vine is unique among morning glory vines because it blooms in the heat of the day rather than in the cool of the morning. It is such a strong vine that it creates lush habitat for small birds, lizards, and mammals. It is a good choice to reintroduce to a disturbed site and will do well on a back fence where there is plenty of room to spread. This plant also produces cyanide compounds in its foliage.

Wild potato (*I. pandurata*), with showy white flowers and heart-shaped leaves, is the other member of this group found in the Texas Hill Country.

Rough Leaf Dogwood
Cornus drummondii
Cornaceae

An unevenly shaped shrub or small spreading tree that grows in moist soil along creeks and in bottomlands.

LEAVES: Simple, opposite, deciduous, oval, 1–4 inches long; pointed tip, rough upper surface; leaf veins parallel, elastic, especially prominent on the lower surface.

FLOWERS: Cream-colored on numerous broad, rounded clusters at ends of branches; April–May.

FRUIT: In rounded clusters, small and waxy white with a dark dot; ripens August–October.

RANGE: Central, South, and East Texas; north to Ontario and east to Alabama.

The elastic leaf veins of rough leaf dogwood hold together even after the leaf is broken and pulled apart. Large cream-colored flower clusters make it especially easy to identify in the spring. Rough leaf dogwood in bottomland settings provides good wildlife shelter. It forms thickets; provides visual privacy; produces food for small mammals and many birds, including turkeys and quail; and has abundant spring blossoms. It is a host plant to the azure blue butterfly.

Rough leaf dogwood is a less showy but attractive cousin of the exquisite, well-known flowering dogwood (*C. florida*). The common name "dogwood" is from an English species whose bark was boiled to make a bath to kill mites that caused mange on dogs.

Buffalo Gourd, Stinking Gourd, Calabazilla
Cucurbita foetidissima
Cucurbitaceae

A prostrate vine up to 20 feet long common in disturbed places such as roadsides and fallow fields, with an unpleasant aroma.

LEAVES: Large, up to 12 inches long, arrow-shaped, gray-green; edges with fine teeth, curl upward.

FLOWERS: Yellow, 3–4 inches long, 1–2 inches wide; open in early morning; May–September.

FRUIT: Large, round, green-striped gourd, 3–4 inches wide; turns yellow with age.

RANGE: Southwestern and midwestern United States and Florida.

Buffalo gourd is an herbaceous perennial with a large root. Buffalo gourd is included here because it is an interesting but unappreciated vine. The seeds contain 30–35 percent protein and up to 34 percent oil, and the roots are a source of starch. Native Americans used the seed for food and the fruit to make soap. Buffalo gourd lives up to forty years and has a huge, starchy root that can weigh about 65 pounds after only two growing seasons. It is currently being investigated as a source of starch and oil for commercial use.

Texas Persimmon, Mexican Persimmon
Diospyros texana
Ebenaceae
Common shrub or small tree that grows in thickets, open woodlands, hillsides, and ravines; easily recognized by its smooth, gray trunks and branches.
LEAVES: Simple, alternate; dark green above and gray-green below; leathery, with smooth edges that roll under.
FLOWERS: Small, fragrant, white bells; hang singly or in small clusters among new leaves; February–June.
FRUIT: Green turning blue-black when ripe; round and fleshy, about 1 inch in diameter with abundant rain but usually smaller; male and female flowers on separate plants, so only some have fruit; sweet and edible when ripe from late July–September.

BARK: Smooth, light gray, thin; sometimes peels off in small, thin, rectangular flakes.
RANGE: Western two-thirds of Texas into northern Mexico.

The fruit of the female tree is eaten by many birds and mammals, including turkeys, coyotes, raccoon, and javelinas. Deer and goats browse both the leaves and fruit. Where they are thick, Texas persimmons can provide good nest sites for the tiny, rare black-capped vireo. This tree is a host plant to gray hairstreak and Henry's elfin butterflies.

With its high sugar content, Texas persimmon fruit can be eaten raw, made into jelly, or fermented to make a tasty varietal wine. In Mexico, the black juice of the persimmon is used to dye animal hides. Texas persimmon is in the same family as the African ebony that produces the beautiful black wood used for furniture and piano keys.

Texas Madrone
Arbutus xalapensis
Ericaceae

Uncommon, distinctive, and desirable small evergreen tree with a round open crown, stout crooked branches, and very smooth tan or reddish bark. Found on limestone hillsides with Ashe juniper.

LEAVES: Simple, alternate, evergreen; dark green, leathery ovals, 2–5 inches long; most leaves at ends of twigs; young leaf stems usually red.

FLOWERS: Small, white, urn-shaped in elongated, woolly clusters; March.

FRUIT: Small, round, red; in clusters, edible.

BARK: Conspicuous, thin pink to reddish brown, peeling in papery layers and exposing white to reddish inner bark.

RANGE: Central Texas, West Texas, and the Texas Panhandle; southeastern New Mexico, Mexico, and Guatemala.

The name madrone comes from the Spanish word *madrona,* which means "strawberry tree." Grazing and heavy browsing by white-tailed deer have caused a decrease in the Texas madrone populations of Central Texas. Its flowers, fruit, unique shape, and bark make this tree a beautiful ornamental, but it can be difficult to propagate. The red fruit is sweet and popular with many birds and small mammals. The wood is hard and has been used for tool handles and gunpowder charcoal. Its bark and roots can be used to make yellow, orange, and brown dyes. In Mexico, the leaves are sometimes used as an astringent or a diuretic.

Bill Ward

Southwest Bernardia, Myrtle Croton, Oreja de Raton
Bernardia myricifolia
Euphorbiaceae

A dense, thornless shrub, 3 to 8 feet tall, with many branches and younger parts that are very hairy.

LEAVES: Small, dark green, simple, alternate, with wavy margins and obscure veins on topside; underside lighter with dense, starlike hairs and prominent veins.

FLOWERS: Small and inconspicuous; male and female flowers may be on the same plant or different plants.

FRUIT: Green to grayish brown, $\frac{1}{3}$–$\frac{1}{2}$ inch, globelike with 3 obvious chambers and 1 seed in each.

TWIGS: Slender and mostly short; when young are green to grayish and covered with starlike hairs; when older are gray and hairless.

RANGE: South Central and South-Texas.

Found on dry caliche hills, canyons, and rocky slopes, southwest bernardia commonly grows in association with cenizo and Texas kidneywood. This plant is very drought tolerant and used by wildlife in many ways. Doves, cardinals, sparrows, and quail eat the seeds. It is a host plant for Lacey's Scrub-Hairstreak butterfly. Deer love southwest bernardia and in areas of deer overpopulation, it is browsed down to a stunted dwarf. The Spanish name, *oreja de raton*, refers to the leaves, which look like little mouse ears.

Bush Croton, Encinilla, Hierba Loca
Croton fruticulosus
Euphorbiaceae

A low, deciduous, aromatic shrub with slender, arched, and leafy branches; found in brush on limestone hills, bluffs, and canyons from eastern edge of the Hill Country westward.

LEAVES: Simple, alternate, up to 3 inches long; oval with pointed tips, edges smooth or with very fine teeth; soft hairs on gray-green lower surface; upper surface sometimes smooth and sometimes with soft hair; aromatic when crushed.

FLOWERS: Pale yellow or cream-colored, very small on ends of small terminal branches.

FRUIT: Round, indistinctly 3-lobed; covered with fine, stellate hairs; summer–fall.

RANGE: Central and West Texas, New Mexico, Arizona, and northern Mexico.

Croton is a large genus of about 750 species. Bush crotons are not eaten by livestock (they are poisonous to livestock) and thus increase with overgrazing of other plants. Other croton species in Texas are host plants to the goatweed and gray hairstreak butterflies, and *C. fruticulosus* is probably also a butterfly host plant.

INVASIVE EXOTIC SPECIES

Chinese Tallow Tree
Sapium sebiferum
Euphorbiaceae
Invasive, alien tree common along streams throughout the Texas Hill Country.

LEAVES: Simple, alternate, a little broader than long; with smooth edges and a long pointed tip; turn yellow, orange, and red in autumn.

FLOWERS: Small, yellow, in clusters 2–8 inches long; May–June.

FRUIT: Round, hard, 3-lobed capsule with 1 seed in each lobe, each seed covered in white waxy coating (tallow); ripens in fall and often hangs on tree into the winter.

BARK: Gray-brown, with flat ridges and shallow fissures.

RANGE: From China; introduced into southeastern United States in 1700s and spread throughout Southern states: Texas, Louisiana, Arkansas, Mississippi, Alabama, Georgia, Florida, South Carolina, and North Carolina.

Chinese tallow is cultivated in China for the oil or tallow in its seed, which is used for soap and candles. Here, it is an invasive pioneer plant that quickly spreads into otherwise unspoiled watersheds and fallow fields, where it excludes native plants. When Chinese tallow leaves fall to the ground, they release a cyanogenic compound capable of inhibiting growth of other plants, which helps make this tree an effective invader. Look at the leaf shape and seed for easy identification. Also, it is easy to identify in autumn when it turns color.

Bill Ward Bill Ward

Huisache
Acacia minuata
(A. farnesiana)
Fabaceae

A small, spiny, round tree with bright yellow-gold spring blossoms that reaches the northernmost part of its range on the southern and southeastern edges of the Hill Country, where it is often shrublike with many narrow trunks.

LEAVES: Alternate, doubly compound with 10–18 pairs of tiny slender leaflets; distinct, fine, feathery foliage on branches with paired spines at leaf nodes.

FLOWERS: Numerous, bright yellow-gold, ½-inch balls that give the tree a showy golden hue; strong, sweet aroma; March–April.

FRUIT: Woody legume pods, 1–2 inches long, brown to black; each pod with 2 rows of shiny, hard gray seeds; often eaten by weevils; midsummer to early fall.

RANGE: In south-central and South Texas east to Florida, west to Arizona, and south into northern South America.

Huisache (often pronounced "WEE-satch") is designated by the Texas Department of Transportation as an invasive plant that needs special control measures. This fast-growing, drought-resistant pioneer shrub naturally moves into sunny, disturbed areas, such as pastures. On the northern edge of its range, huisache is not such a problem as in other areas. On newly disturbed ground, it can provide quick shade and protection for many plants. Bees make tasty honey from its flowers, and birds eat its seeds.

Huisache branches are armed with long, tough spines. The blossoms are used to make perfume, and the pods have been used to make ink. The juice produces a glue used to mend pottery. In parts of Mexico, crushed leaves are made into wound dressings, and the flowers are used in an ointment to soothe headaches.

Catclaw, Roemer's Acacia
Acacia roemeriana
Fabaceae

Southwestern, dryland, prickly shrub with many spreading branches (occasionally a small tree) that grows onto the southern edge of the Edwards Plateau.

LEAVES: Doubly compound, with 4–8 pairs of leaflets, ½–⅗ inch long.

FLOWERS: Fluffly, cream-colored balls, about ½ inch wide; on 1-inch-long, purple-red stems; April–May.

FRUIT: Flat pod, about 3 inches long and 1 inch wide, brown to reddish.

BARK AND TWIGS: Bark smooth at first and, when older, with small scales; twigs with short, curved, thornlike prickles.

RANGE: From Central Texas south and west to El Paso, southern New Mexico, and northern Mexico; also Baja California; common around New Braunfels, San Antonio, Langtry, and Del Rio.

The species is named for Ferdinand Roemer, who was a German scientist-explorer in Texas in 1845–47. He collected specimens around New Braunfels. *Roemer's Texas,* the English translation of his early Texas travels and observations, is available online.

Catclaw is usually 3–10 feet tall. The largest catclaw grows in Comal County, is 17 feet tall, and has a trunk circumference of 26 inches. Catclaw is a host plant for Reakirt's blue and Mexican sulphur (Mexican yellow) butterflies.

Two other Texas species are commonly called catclaw, *A. wrightii* and *A. greggii,* and they might be found on the southernmost edge of the Hill Country. Their blossoms, unlike those of *A. roemeriana,* are longer than wide.

False Indigo
Amorpha fruticosa
Fabaceae

An attractive, open shrub with several stems sometimes found in light shade on upper portion of stream banks.

LEAVES: Deciduous, pinnately compound, with 9–29 oval leaflets, about 1 inch long; with smooth edges and upper surface.

FLOWERS: Numerous spikes, 2–4 inches long, dark blue to reddish purple with gold to orange anthers; April–May.

FRUIT: Small pods, less than ½ inch long; dotted by glands visible with a hand lens.

RANGE: Moist woods or limestone stream banks throughout Texas, west to California, and north and east to Minnesota and New Hampshire.

Indiscriminate clearing along streams is reducing the occurrence of this plant in the Texas Hill Country. It grows well in soil with poor drainage and is important in streamside erosion control. Look for this plant, and protect it or add it to a riparian planting mix.

False indigo is also a popular native landscape plant in areas with some moisture and light shade to full sun. Its tall, dark blossom spikes are a fine contrast to other more flowery blossoms.

Its odd genus name, *Amorpha*, means "without form" and refers to the tiny flowers on the blossom spikes. Each little flower has only one petal instead of five, which is common in some other members of the legume family. False indigo is a host plant to the gray hairstreak, silver-spotted skipper, marine blue, and southern dogface butterflies.

Texas Redbud
Cercis canadensis var. *texensis*
Fabaceae

A popular drought-tolerant native that grows in full sun or part shade. Small tree with distinctive heart-shaped leaves and pink flowers in early spring.

LEAVES: Alternate, simple, deciduous, heart-shaped.

FLOWERS: Rose-pink, pealike blossoms; in clusters, on older branches and often along the trunk; appear before and as the leaves emerge; March–April.

FRUIT: In clusters of shiny, reddish brown, flat legume seed pods 2–4 inches long; ripens in the fall.

BARK: Smooth, thin, and reddish brown when young; turns gray and scaly with narrow ridges when older.

RANGE: Texas Hill Country variety found in Central Texas and in limited areas of Oklahoma and Mexico.

Texas redbud is the most popular small native tree for landscaping in the Hill Country. It grows fast, has few pests, and tolerates drought. It can easily be overlooked during winter months when leaves and flowers are missing.

In the wild, redbud is one of the first plants to resprout after a fire. When buying one at a nursery, make sure it is a Texas redbud rather than an Eastern redbud. The latter is not as hardy in the Hill Country limestone soil and dry climate. The flower buds, flowers, and new tender seed pods are edible and a gourmet treat when sautéed in butter. Fresh flowers are also good in salads. Texas redbud is a host plant for the Henry's elfin butterfly.

Black Dalea
Dalea frutescens
Fabaceae

Low, loose, rounded bush with tiny
leaves and bright purple blossoms;
found on sunny, dry, rocky roadsides,
slopes, and fields.

LEAVES: Compound, with 9–17 tiny,
grayish green leaflets with minute
glands on the underside.

FLOWERS: Bright purple, pea-shaped,
in dense heads; after a good rain,
bush can become a mass of color
that lasts 1–2 weeks; July–October.

FRUIT: Inconspicuous, flattened capsule with 1–2 seeds.

RANGE: In Texas from the Colorado
River west and south to the Rio
Grande; also in southeastern New
Mexico and northern Mexico.

Black dalea was once more common
and a good drought-resistant browse
for livestock. Quickly eliminated by
cattle, it is now absent from much
of its former range. Black dalea can
be an outstanding low-growing,
drought-tolerant, landscape shrub
that is especially attractive in mass
plantings.

Texas Kidneywood
Eysenhardtia texana
Fabaceae

Medium to tall shrub with many trunks and an irregular shape; common on dry limestone soil in sun or partial shade.

LEAVES: Alternate, pinnately compound, not more than 3½ inches long, with 13–47 tiny leaflets that have a pungent aroma when crushed; drop during drought but return after rain.

FLOWERS: Small, fragrant, white blossoms on short, 1¼-inch flower spikes at ends of small branches; in May and intermittent after rains through the summer and fall.

FRUIT: Small pods, often with a short thread at the tip end; growing along small spikes at the ends of short branches.

RANGE: Primarily in the Hill Country of the Edwards Plateau; also on limestone soils in South Texas, the Trans-Pecos, and parts of northern Mexico.

Kidneywood is a good landscape plant that can be pruned into a small, attractive, flowering tree that grows fast with extra watering but is drought tolerant when established. The specimen originally used to describe and name *E. texana* was collected in New Braunfels. The common name is derived from a very closely related Mexican species used to treat kidney and bladder disorders. The wood, when steeped in water, produces first yellow and then orange colors, and the water, when held against a black background, shows a surprising blue fluorescence. Kidneywood blossoms produce excellent bee forage, and the leaves are good deer browse. It is a host plant to the southern dogface butterfly.

Golden Ball Lead Tree
Leucaena retusa
Fabaceae

A loose shrub or small tree with bright, gold flowers all summer; grows in dry, rocky limestone soil of southwestern Edwards Plateau and common on roadsides and hillsides around Garner State Park near Leakey.

LEAVES: Bipinnately compound, with 3–8 pairs of oblong, blue-green leaflets ½–¾ inch long.

FLOWERS: Plentiful, bright yellow-gold balls, about 1 inch wide; April and then sporadically until October.

FRUIT: Thin, papery, narrow brown pods, 4–10 inches long.

BARK: Gray to brown, smooth on young growth and thin scale on old trunks.

RANGE: Southwestern Edwards Plateau, the Trans-Pecos, southern New Mexico, and northern Mexico.

Native plant gardeners like to plant this small tree in sunny spots with rocky soil. The common, multiple stems can be pruned to produce a tree with a single trunk. Golden ball lead tree is well adapted to poor soil on hot, dry exposures and is especially attractive in the spring when it explodes with eye-catching blossoms. Deer and livestock browse this plant heavily; butterflies and bees feed on its nectar.

Pink Mimosa
Mimosa borealis
Fabaceae

Usually a low shrub with many branches that grows in dry limestone along country roads, on hillsides, and in open brushy places.

LEAVES: Small, double-pinnately compound, with tiny, oval leaflets, only about ⅛ inch long.

FLOWERS: Fragrant, showy, pink globes about ½ inch in diameter; March–May.

FRUIT: A flat legume pod 1–2 inches long, more or less constricted between 2–7 seeds; may be a few stout prickles on margin of seed pod.

RANGE: Trans-Pecos and Edwards Plateau in Texas; also Oklahoma, New Mexico, and northern Mexico.

Pink mimosa has many small straight or recurved prickles, or "catclaws," along its branches. In spring, this inconspicuous shrub becomes a bright splash of pink because of its fluffy, ball-shaped blossoms. With its showy blossoms, pink mimosa is a beautiful plant in full flower and a wonderful dry-landscape ornamental available in some native plant nurseries. The fragrant blossoms attract many types of butterflies, and its seeds are eaten by birds. This attractive shrub is most common south of a line drawn between Menard and Austin.

Retama, Paloverde
Parkinsonia aculeata
Fabaceae

Small, open tree or large shrub, with distinct green bark on slender spiny branches commonly found in pastures, fallow fields, and other disturbed places.

LEAVES: Slender, bright green, 10–16 inches long, compound with 20–30 pairs of leaflets; each leaf guarded by 3 sharp spines at its base; grow in bunches that look like plumes; early deciduous.

FLOWERS: Bright yellow turning orange; fragrant in loose clusters among the leaves; April–September.

FRUIT: Pods 2–4 inches long with constrictions, with 1–8 seeds; seeds mature in July.

RANGE: From the southern edge of the Edwards Plateau throughout South Texas west to Arizona and south to South America.

Retama is a southern plant and throughout its range has many local names and uses. It is grown as an ornamental and used for making paper. In Mexico, a grove of retama is called a *retamal.* In tropical America, retama has been reported in medicinal use to reduce fever, induce abortions, and treat diabetes and epilepsy. In some places, the flowers are important honeybee forage, and the seeds are eaten by birds.

Honey Mesquite, Mesquite
Prosopis glandulosa var. *glandulosa*
Fabaceae

Thorny, small tree with an open crown, drooping branches, and narrow leaflets; found on many different sites but often invasive and abundant in fallow fields and abandoned pastures, reaching its greatest size in rich bottomland near streams.

LEAVES: Alternate, deciduous, doubly compound, up to 10 inches long, on branches having gray spines.

FLOWERS: Yellow-green on long spike, grouped in small clusters; spring, but also summer with good rain.

FRUIT: Narrow, tan legume pods 4–10 inches long, growing in clusters; seeds brown and shiny, set in spongy material; seeds ripen in August–September.

BARK: Rough, reddish brown to gray, with deep fissures and thick ridges when mature.

RANGE: Across Texas west to New Mexico, north to Kansas and Arkansas, east to Louisiana, and south to northern Mexico.

Extremely common, honey mesquite is on the Texas Department of Transportation's list of plants that are invasive and need control. It now covers millions of acres and forms dense thickets that limit land use. In moderation, mesquite can be appreciated for many important uses. As a legume, the tree fixes nitrogen, thus enriching the soil. Mesquite is excellent firewood for cooking, and the wood is also used for flooring, furniture, and gunstocks. Bees make honey from its blossoms; and many species of wildlife, including deer and dove, depend on mesquite for food and shelter. Mesquite is a host plant for Reakirt's blue, and ceraunus blue butterflies. Mesquite beans can be an important food source for horses, cattle, and goats.

Eve's Necklace
Sophora affinis
Fabaceae

Spindly shrub or graceful small tree recognized by its smooth green twigs and in fall and winter by the dark "beads-in-a-chain" seed pods.

LEAVES: Deciduous, compound, with 13–19 narrow, oval leaflets each 1 inch long; in pairs with 1 at terminal end.

FLOWERS: Fragrant, pale pink, pea-shaped blossoms hanging in large clusters; March–May.

FRUIT: Black leathery pod containing 1–8 shiny brown seeds, very narrow between seeds; thin fleshy walls with extremely unpleasant taste; often remains on tree through winter.

BARK: Gray-green on young trees; fairly smooth, becoming rough with thin scales and shallow longitudinal lines.

RANGE: In a band from Central Texas north to the Red River; also in southwestern Oklahoma and northwestern Louisiana.

Found in open woods, along fence-rows, and in thickets, this slender tree is most attractive when given some space to develop an even, rounded crown. Pretty spring blossoms and a pleasing shape in winter, with branches decorated by black beadlike seed pods, make this plant an excellent ornamental.

Texas Mountain Laurel, Mescalbean
Sophora secundiflora
Fabaceae

An evergreen shrub or small tree frequently found on limestone hillsides; grows scattered and in association with Ashe juniper (mountain cedar) and Spanish oak.

LEAVES: Shiny, dark green, compound; with 5–13 oval leaflets each 1–2 inches long, paired, with 1 on terminal end.

FLOWERS: Beautiful, aromatic blue-purple clusters; smell like grape flavoring; individual flowers shaped like a pea blossom; February–April.

FRUIT: Hard, silver-gray seed pod 3–5 inches long, containing 1–8 bright orange seeds; seeds ripen in September.

RANGE: Central Texas, West Texas, and into southern New Mexico; South Texas through northern Mexico.

Texas mountain laurel is a slow-growing ornamental shrub or small tree that can be grown from scarified (scratched with a file) seed. Fresh pink seeds sprout more readily than older dried seeds that are bright red or orange and very hard. This tree is not the same mountain laurel as that of the eastern United States, *Kalmia latifolia,* or the true laurel of Asia and the Mediterranean, *Laureus nobilis.*

The leaves and seeds of Texas mountain laurel contain a toxic alkaloid that is poisonous to cattle, sheep, goats, and humans. If broken or chewed, the seeds can be fatal to a human. When swallowed by a child, however, they usually remain intact and pass through the digestive tract, causing no harm. Texas mountain laurel is a host plant to Henry's elfin and orange sulphur butterflies.

Spanish Oak, Texas Red Oak
Quercus buckleyi (Q. texana)
Fagaceae

Small to medium sized, often multi-trunked tree on limestone hillsides across the Texas Hill Country in association with Ashe juniper, live oak, Lacey oak, and black cherry.

LEAVES: Simple, alternate, deciduous, 5 ½ inches long or less; with deep narrow lobes having fairly long points or bristles at the outer ends.

FLOWERS: Male and female catkins on same tree, 1–3 ½ inches long; male hairy and female with reddish color; early spring.

FRUIT: Small, oval acorns, about ¾ inch long; red-brown with short soft hairs and often with thin dark stripes; ripen September–October.

BARK: Dark gray-brown with plate-like scales and deep fissures, or sometimes gray and smooth.

RANGE: Central Texas to the Pecos River; also in the Arbuckle Mountains in southern Oklahoma.

Spanish oak produces beautiful fall foliage in various shades of rich red. It provides an abundant acorn crop that feeds deer, turkeys, squirrels, and scrub-jays and is a host plant to skipper and hairstreak butterflies. The rare golden-cheeked warbler, endemic to the Texas Hill Country, depends on this tree for food and nesting.

Spanish oak is highly susceptible to oak wilt, which is killing many Hill Country oaks. Fungal mats form in the Spanish oaks and attract beetles that feed on them and then carry the fungal spores to other oaks, including live oaks, thus spreading the disease.

Lacey Oak, Blue Oak
Quercus laceyi (Q. glaucoides)
Fagaceae

Small- to medium-sized tree that grows only on limestone hills and canyons.

LEAVES: Simple, alternate, late deciduous, leathery; dull, dark blue-green above and lower surface paler, sometimes yellow or pink the fall; 2–5 inches long with round, wavy lobes.

FLOWERS: Male catkins 2–2 ½ inches long; female catkins minute; spring.

FRUIT: Brown acorns in clusters with flattened ends.

BARK: Dark gray to brown in long, narrow fissures; with small, square plates on older trees.

RANGE: Confined to Edwards Plateau in Texas; also in northeastern Mexico.

To find the Lacey oak, a beautiful and tough tree, look carefully at the smaller oaks growing in rocky places. From a distance, Lacey oaks have a distinct smoky, dark blue-gray appearance. This oak is becoming a popular landscape tree for the Hill Country because it is resistant to drought and oak wilt, is well adapted to alkaline soil, and has attractive, smoky blue leaves that may produce late fall color. The Lacey oak is named for Howard Lacey, a rancher who discovered this tree on his land near Kerrville.

Steve Nelle

Bur Oak
Quercus macrocarpa
Fagaceae

Majestic shade tree found in the deep soil of river valleys noted for its great height, wide crown, and distinctively large leaves and acorns.

LEAVES: Huge, alternate, simple, with deep lobes; leaf shape widest near outer end, shiny dark green above and paler below; deciduous.

FLOWERS: Male catkins 4–6 inches long; April–May.

FRUIT: Large acorns up to 2 inches across in a thick fringed cup; August–September.

TWIGS: Thick and gray-brown or reddish, often with corky wings along small branches.

BARK: Thick corky bark with prominent parallel ridges and deep furrows in between.

RANGE: From Canada south to Gulf Coast states and from Great Plains to East Coast; uncommon in, and probably only introduced to, the Texas Hill Country. Acorn size and extent of cup fringe appears to increase from north to south.

Bur oak is a popular, ornamental shade tree that grows fairly fast and is tolerant of drought, heat, cold, insects, and fire. It prefers neutral, deep, well-drained soil. Bur oak acorns are excellent food for small and large mammals and many birds. The tiny insects on these trees attract many insectivorous songbirds, and the tree itself is a good nest site for songbirds and hummingbirds.

The common name "bur" is supposed to describe the fringed acorn, which might look a little like the spiny bur of a chestnut. Bur oak wood produces one of the best and most durable oak lumbers. Native Americans gathered the acorns in late fall and buried them for use in the winter or spring when they were boiled, split, and eaten; boiled, mashed, and eaten with grease; or roasted in hot ashes and eaten. Native Americans also once used the inner bark for medicinal purposes. It was mixed with extractions from other medicinal plants to treat lung troubles and pinworms, to wrap broken bones, and as an astringent and heart remedy.

Blackjack Oak
Quercus marilandica
Fagaceae

Relatively small deciduous oak with rounded crown that grows to about 30 feet on dry gravel or sandy soil.

LEAVES: Simple, alternate, widest at the upper end, leathery, shiny above and hairy below; wedge-shaped with tiny bristle points at end of 3, sometimes indistinct lobes; turning dark red-brown in late fall; many leaves often held on tree through winter.

FLOWERS: Male catkins 2–4 inches long; female catkins tiny, less than ¼ inch long; appear with new leaves in spring.

FRUIT: Small acorns up to ¾ inch long with nearly half of acorn enclosed in its seed cup, solitary or in pairs, mature in 2 years; late fall or early winter.

BARK: Dark, broken into rough, blocky plates.

RANGE: Central Texas is far south-western corner of its range; north to Minnesota, east to Florida, and northeast to New York.

Blackjack oaks are associated with post oak, and this mixture is common throughout much of Central Texas. It grows slowly and is difficult to transplant; thus, it is not particularly popular at native tree nurseries, although it is an excellent small shade tree. Blackjack oak is a host plant to skippers and to hairstreak and admiral butterflies. As with other oaks, the acorns are eaten by deer and turkeys.

Chinkapin Oak, Chinquapin Oak
Quercus muhlenbergii
Fagaceae

A slender, deciduous oak growing on well-drained limestone slopes, near streams, and in canyons where protected from west sun; readily seen growing in association with bigtooth maples in Lost Maples State Park.

LEAVES: Simple, alternate, 4–6 inches long and 1–4 inches wide; oblong with coarse-toothed edges, each tooth with a tiny bristle at the end.

FLOWERS: Male and female blossoms on separate catkins on same tree; male catkins 3–4 inches long; female catkins minute.

FRUIT: Acorns usually single, about 1 inch long and ¾ inch wide; mature in 1 year.

BARK: Pale gray-brown, in narrow, loose plates.

RANGE: Through the eastern half of the United States.

The species name is for G. H. E. Muhlenberg, late-eighteenth-century botanist and minister from Pennsylvania. The leaves of the chinkapin oak are very different from those of other oaks growing in the Texas Hill Country. The wood is dense and long-lasting and has been used for split-rail fences, farm implements, posts, railroad ties, and fuel. Deer, turkeys, squirrels, and raccoon love its relatively sweet acorns.

Shin Oak, White Shin Oak, Bigelow Oak
Quercus sinuata
Fagaceae

Attractive, small deciduous tree up to 30 feet tall in deep soil but much shorter in the poor upland sites where commonly found.

LEAVES: Alternate, leathery, about 2–3 inches long with wavy edges; may be minute tufts of star-shaped hairs on upper surface, lower surface lighter with soft hairs.

FLOWERS: Male catkins 1–2 inches long; female shorter.

FRUIT: Single or paired acorns, ½–1 inch long with short cap covering only uppermost end.

BARK: Distinct, thin, grayish-tan, flaky.

RANGE: Southern Oklahoma, Central Texas, West Texas, and parts of northern Mexico.

Shin oak is often a tough, small, slender tree growing in very thin limestone soil. On the dry western edge of its range, shin oak will also form shrub thickets. In other sites, where it will grow larger, shin oak may be confused with the Lacey oak. To distinguish it from Lacey oak, whose leaf shape is similar, look closely at the bark. Shin oak bark is very different: thin, light gray, or tan and flaky. An unusually large shin oak tree grows in Austin. It is 39 feet tall with a crown spread of 34 feet.

Post Oak
Quercus stellata
Fagaceae

Medium-sized oak tree with stout limbs and fairly large-lobed leaves; often found in groves on upland sites, providing shade over poor soil.

LEAVES: Simple, alternate, deciduous, leathery, 3–5 inches long with 5 distinct lobes; upper lobes largest and create a cross shape; dark green above, paler below, covered with tiny star-shaped hairs that can be seen with a hand lens.

FLOWERS: Male and female catkins on same tree, but male flowers most obvious, up to 5 inches long; appear in spring with small new leaves.

FRUIT: Acorns in fall solitary, in pairs, or clustered; to 1 inch long, fairly small cup; usually produced every 2–3 years.

BARK: Thin and scaly when young; thick with dark gray ridges separated by deep longitudinal fissures on mature trees.

RANGE: From Central Texas north to Kansas and New England and east to Florida.

The post oak is an extremely common tree throughout the eastern two-thirds of Texas. Locally, it often grows in association with blackjack oak. It is found with hickory north and east of the area covered by this book. Although considered an inferior species by some, this oak thrives in different soil types and is resistant to the oak wilt fungus, fire damage, drought, and injury from lawn equipment. It also provides valuable food for wildlife such as deer and turkeys. Covered with an inch of firm moist soil, the acorns are easy to sprout either in fall or spring. This species hybridizes freely and has produced a number of varieties and hybrids in other parts of Texas and other states, where it is known by various common names.

Live Oak, Plateau Live Oak
Quercus virginiana var. *fusiformis (Q. fusiformis)*
Fagaceae

The signature tree of the Texas Hill Country, well-known and much loved for its massive limbs and distinctive contours.

LEAVES: Simple, alternate, evergreen; thick, narrow ovals, dark green above and paler below; edges smooth and somewhat downcurved, 1–3 inches long; young seedlings may have pointed, lobed leaves; drop off in the spring usually just before new leaves appear.

FLOWERS: Male and female catkins on same tree, male yellow and female with some red; spring.

FRUIT: Acorns fairly slender, about 1 inch long, in small clusters; mature late summer–early fall.

BARK: Gray and smooth at first; dark brown and gray with age; with deep irregular furrows on large trees.

RANGE: From Texas north to Oklahoma and east to Virginia and Florida.

In the Texas Hill Country, live oak leaves are a primary food source for white-tailed deer. Although the leaves' nutritional quality is less than ideal, this tree's overwhelming abundance and persistent green leaves offset the low quality. Because of the great number of live oaks, especially in years with high production, their acorns are also an important food for turkeys, jays, titmice, and woodpeckers. It is a host plant to skippers and to hairstreak and admiral butterflies.

The Hill Country population of live oaks is now being reduced by oak wilt, which is spreading slowly but persistently, especially in urban and suburban areas where trees are commonly wounded and made vulnerable to infection. Although the disease can be controlled to some extent, treatment is arduous and expensive. Consequently, other species such as bur oak, Lacey oak, cedar elm, pecan, walnut, red mulberry, and sycamore, should be planted in the place of live oaks wherever possible.

Lindheimer's Silktassel
Garrya ovata subsp. *lindheimeri (G. lindheimeri)*
Garryaceae

A beautiful evergreen shrub or small tree with large, dark green leaves that are outstanding in the winter; found frequently on rocky slopes, ledges, and bluffs, as well as along streambeds and in ravines.

LEAVES: Simple, opposite, evergreen, fuzzy, somewhat leathery, dark green, up to 2 ½ inches long; variable shape but usually oval with a very small, abrupt tip, with smooth edges.

FLOWERS: Male and female flowers on different plants; female flowers on attractive, drooping, dusty pink clusters; March–April.

FRUIT: Small, dark blue, somewhat fleshy and round with a short tip and a white coating that is easily rubbed off; grows in elongated clumps from the base of new leaves.

RANGE: Edwards Plateau of Central Texas, the Trans-Pecos, and Mexico.

This genus consists of eighteen species found only in North America. Lindheimer's silktassel is unique to the Texas Hill Country and the Trans-Pecos region. The genus was named for Nicholas Garry, once secretary of the Hudson's Bay Company. Abundant fruit on the female plants is an important food source for birds and small mammals. Silktassel appears to be a good native shrub for landscaping, but it is not generally available in nurseries. Some local growers are currently experimenting with its propagation.

Witch Hazel
Hamamelis virginiana
Hamamelidaceae

Little-known and rare large shrub or small understory tree; preferring the rich, moist soil of deep, shady, protected canyons with water.

LEAVES: Simple, deciduous, 2–5 inches long, growing nearly opposite on short branches off a main branch; broad ovals with the widest part and wavy-lobed edges beyond the middle; most leaves smooth, but fuzzy on new growth and young plants; many leaf stems in small zigzag shape due to bud scars.

FLOWERS: Small, yellow, spidery; fall–early winter.

FRUIT: Pale, roundish seed capsules, ½ inch long, set in acornlike cups; present with flowers; 1–2 shiny, black seeds per capsule ejected explosively upon drying.

RANGE: From Bandera County of Central Texas east to Georgia and north to Minnesota and Quebec.

In the Texas Hill Country, witch hazel is known from isolated locations in Bandera and Kerr counties. You can see this wonderful tree growing in association with the bigtooth maple at Lost Maples State Park in Real County. The common name comes from the fact that the forked branches of this tree were once a favorite for "water witching." An aromatic extraction from witch hazel leaves, twigs, and bark is used as a mild astringent for cuts, bruises, and insect bites. It is a pretty, shade-loving landscape plant in moist, well-drained soil. Witch hazel grows fairly fast, and its leaves produce bright yellow fall color. Witch hazel is easy to grow and should be available from native plant growers.

Texas Buckeye
Aesculus glabra var. *arguta*
Hippocastanaceae

A large shrub or small tree 10–30 feet tall adapted to both granite and limestone soil; found in scattered locations in Kerr and Gillespie counties.

LEAVES: Compound, 7–11 inches long, dark green; with slender leaflets radiating from a central point, edges with fine teeth.

FLOWERS: Pale yellow to yellow-green with a dab of red, about ½ inch long, in clusters; March–April.

FRUIT: Black seeds in a spiny capsule.

RANGE: From Texas north through Iowa and Nebraska.

Texas buckeye does well in or near streambeds. It is an eye-catching small tree or shrub that does well in full sun and can be used in native plant landscape gardening.

Pale Buckeye, Yellow Buckeye
Aesculus pavia var. *flavescens*
Hippocastanaceae

Yellow-flowered variety of the red buckeye unique to the Edwards Plateau, especially in thickets and drainages of Kendall, Kerr, Bandera, Uvalde, Real, southern Blanco, and western Comal counties.

LEAVES: Opposite, palmately compound, usually with 5 large leaflets.

FLOWERS: Yellow, tubular, in an upright cluster 4–8 inches long; appear with new leaves; March–May.

FRUIT: Round, brown capsule with 2-inch diameter that persists after leaves are gone, containing 1–3 shiny, brown seeds with a white "eye"; seeds poisonous; summer.

RANGE: Edwards Plateau west to Edwards County.

Pale buckeye is a symmetrical understory bush that leafs out in early spring and drops its leaves when it goes dormant in the heat of the summer. The flowers are an important early spring nectar source for hummingbirds. Because they remain dormant and therefore unidentified from midsummer through fall and winter into early spring, many of these unique Hill Country shrubs are being cleared with the cedar. They are found only in a small area, and they have showy, yellow blossoms, two reasons that make pale buckeye worth protecting. Native Americans used the seeds and leaves, which are poisonous, to stun and catch fish in ponds and slow-moving streams. The bark contains aesculin, a compound that absorbs UV rays and is used in some sunscreens.

The red buckeye (*A. pavia* var. *pavia*) occurs in eastern and southeastern Texas as well as on the eastern edge of the Texas Hill County in Travis, Hays, Comal, and Bexar counties, where it sometimes hybridizes with the pale buckeye to produce plants with pink or reddish blossoms.

Canyon Mock Orange
Philadelphus ernestii
Hydrangeaceae

A rare, low, open shrub with fragrant, white blossoms; found growing near springs, among boulders, and on bluffs in moist, shady canyons.

LEAVES: Simple, opposite, slender, deciduous, about 1 ½ inches long; 3 distinct veins and a few short straight hairs above, but with dense short hairs pressed flat against the lower leaf surface.

FLOWERS: Showy, 4 white petals with numerous yellow stamens in the center, fragrant; April–May.

FRUIT: A very small, not quite globe-shaped capsule.

RANGE: Endemic to the Texas Hill Country.

Canyon mock orange is listed by the state as a "Species of Concern" and is in need of protection. It is found only in Kendall, Comal, Blanco, Hays, and Travis counties. An almost identical and also uncommon species is *P. texensis,* found in Bandera, Edwards, Real, and Uvalde counties. If you find any of these shrubs, be sure to note their location, protect, and monitor them.

Pecan
Carya illinoinensis
Juglandaceae

Towering shade tree with broad crown and tall, straight trunk often found growing naturally on rich bottomland near rivers and streams.

LEAVES: Alternate, deciduous, compound, up to 1 ½ feet long; with 4–8 pairs of opposite leaflets and 1 at tip end; leaflets smooth and asymmetrical with small teeth, allowing them to hang vertically and shed rainwater.

FLOWERS: Male and female on same tree; male flower spike or catkin 5–6 inches long; spring.

FRUIT: Elongate, thin-shelled nuts covered by green husk drying to dark brown; often in clusters of 2–3; nuts mature October–November.

BARK: Usually gray-brown with large, flat scales and narrow, irregular grooves.

RANGE: Native of Oklahoma, Texas, and Louisiana and north to Illinois, Indiana, and Ohio.

The pecan is the state tree of Texas. It was first cultivated in the East in 1766 by Thomas Jefferson at Monticello. He gave some seeds to George Washington, and the trees from these seeds are the oldest now growing at Mount Vernon.

Pecans are excellent high-energy, high-protein food for deer, turkeys, squirrels, and other small mammals. The tree is a host plant for hairstreak butterflies and the cecropia moth. Large pecan bottomlands are the most commonly used turkey roosts in the Hill Country and are thus critically important to that bird's survival in this area. The pecan, whose name comes from an Algonquian word, was an important food source for many Native American groups. The leaves and bark have been used medicinally as an astringent.

Little Walnut, Texas Walnut, Nogal
Juglans microcarpa
Juglandaceae

Usually a small, multitrunked tree found in ravines and near springs, creeks, and rivers.

LEAVES: Alternate, deciduous, compound, to 1 foot long; with 5–12 pairs of leaflets and sometimes 1 at tip end; leaflets narrow, slightly curved with fine or almost no teeth on edges.

FLOWERS: Male and female on same tree; tiny green female flowers at ends of green twigs; male catkins 2–3 inches long, hanging down from smallest twigs; spring.

FRUIT: Single or multiple, in green husk drying to dark brown, total diameter 1 inch or less; nuts dark brown, grooved, and very small.

BARK: Gray-brown, flat, narrow, broken scales; narrow, irregular grooves.

RANGE: Scattered across Texas, Oklahoma, New Mexico, and northern Mexico.

Without nuts, little walnut can be mistaken for an immature pecan, but walnut has smaller leaves and a chambered pith in its small twigs. Little walnut is cultivated in Europe as an ornamental and in the United States for shelter-belt planting. Indians made spears from its branches, and later, settlers used it for fence posts. Juice of the husks will kill ringworm fungus and was used as a dark brown dye by both Native Americans and settlers. Walnut trees are important stabilizers of gravel washes in scoured stream bottoms. Walnut trees are host plants for hairstreak butterflies. Its nuts are eaten by squirrels and javelinas.

Spicebush
Lindera benzoin
Lauraceae

A large shrub or small tree that grows in shade on moist alluvial soil near streams and springs; easily recognized by the citrus aroma of a crushed leaf.

LEAVES: Simple, alternate, a little waxy, bright green on top and paler below; may turn a clear lemon yellow in fall.

FLOWERS: Male and female flowers often on different plants; small, fragrant, yellow, in tiny clusters; appear before the leaves in early spring.

FRUIT: Bright red or less commonly yellow, either solitary or in small clusters, often only on female plants; ripens in late summer and fall.

RANGE: From Central Texas, Oklahoma, and Arkansas east to Florida and Virginia and north to Maine, Ontario, and Michigan.

Spicebush berries attract many birds. It is a host plant to spicebush swallowtail and tiger swallowtail butterflies. In November, lemon yellow spicebush leaves stand out like a woodland light bulb. The leaves and fruit of this aromatic shrub make a fragrant, lemon-flavored herb tea. The bark is pleasant to chew, and its berries were once made into a substitute for allspice.

Turk's Cap, Texas Mallo, Drummond's Wax Mallo
Malvaviscus drummondii
Malvaceae

A big, large-leafed perennial, woody only near its base, with bright red blossoms much of the summer and fall; prefers moist, shady sites near streams and springs.

LEAVES: Large, simple, alternate, with palmate veins conspicuous especially on the lower surface, which also has velvety hairs; coarse teeth on edges; shaped like a broad heart or with 3 shallow lobes.

FLOWERS: Showy red petals closed and overlapping with a long "tongue" protruding; look similar to hibiscus buds; June–October.

FRUIT: Fleshy, red, 5-lobed capsule, ½–¾ inch in diameter; August–September.

RANGE: From southern portion of the Texas Hill Country east to Florida and the West Indies; south into Mexico.

Along with many beautiful wildflowers, such as winecup and rose mallow, Turk's cap is in the mallow family. Though somewhat invasive, it is a good shade-tolerant ornamental that can be pruned every other year to control its spread. Turk's cap is readily propagated from seed or green cuttings. The leaves can be made into a poultice for use as a soothing emollient, and its flowers are used medicinally in Mexico to promote menstrual flow. The blossoms are an important nectar source for butterflies and the ruby-throated hummingbird on its fall migration from the northeastern United States through Texas and into Mexico. The small, mealy red fruit is edible either cooked or raw and is food for many birds and mammals.

Bill Ward

Rose Pavonia, Wright Pavonia, Rock Rose
Pavonia lasiopetala
Malvaceae

Small shrub with lovely pink blossoms; mostly herbaceous above and woody toward the base, found occasionally in open dry woods and bluffs.

LEAVES: Alternate, velvety, heart-shaped with toothed edges, dark green above and lighter below.

FLOWERS: Showy pink flowers with 5 petals, about 2 inches wide; March–November.

FRUIT: Small, dry capsule with 5 chambers, each containing 1 seed; July–December.

RANGE: Portions of Edwards Plateau, Rio Grande Plains, Trans-Pecos, and Mexico.

Rose pavonia is highly palatable to all livestock and deer. Although common in the native plant nursery trade, its existence in the wild is limited. Before over browsing, this species may have been much more common. A valuable garden plant because of its showy blooms and long blossom period, rose pavonia can be found in local nurseries that stock native plants. It grows in part shade and full sun and requires modest amounts of water and occasional pruning any time between February and October. This species lives 3–4 years and spreads freely by seeds. It can be propagated by cuttings taken in spring or summer.

INVASIVE EXOTIC SPECIES

Chinaberry
Melia azedarach
Meliaceae

An invasive alien tree with a spreading crown and dark green leaves; now found just about everywhere throughout Central Texas and eastward through the southern United States.

LEAVES: Deciduous, dark green, large, bipinnately compound; leaflets 1–2 inches long, smooth on both surfaces, with toothed edges and pointed tips; yellow in fall.

FLOWERS: Plentiful, in long, loose clusters, each with 5 lilac petals with a dark purple center; appear with leaves April–May.

FRUIT: Yellow-tan, in loose drooping clusters, ½–¾ inch wide; poisonous to goats, hogs, and people; persists into next growing season; ripens September–October.

BARK: In seedlings, dark green, thin, and smooth; on mature trunks, dark gray with thick ridges.

RANGE: From Asia; invasive across southern United States.

This fast-growing, invasive alien species has escaped cultivation and is an example of how an alien species, well adapted to soil and climate, can appear to be native and change local habitat. It is common in disturbed soil, lowlands, and riparian thickets. Chinaberry is found in many otherwise pristine Texas Hill Country watersheds.

Carolina Snailseed
Cocculus carolinus
Menispermaceae

Common trailing, thornless vine found growing on fences and brush; with conspicuous clusters of small but brilliant red, berrylike fruit, each with a single seed in the shape of a flat snail shell.

LEAVES: Simple, alternate, triangular to almost heart-shaped; dark green and smooth above, paler below with dense hair.

FLOWERS: Small, greenish, in loose clusters, male and female on different plants; June–August.

FRUIT: Fleshy, bright red, about ¼ inch in diameter; in loose conspicuous clusters; only on female plants; ripens in fall.

RANGE: Texas east to Florida, north to Kansas and Illinois; northern Mexico.

Snailseed vine is an important food source for migrant songbirds. In early spring, a flock of cedar waxwings will feed on a large vine for several days, stripping it clean of the berries before continuing north to their nesting ground. Female plants that produce the abundant red berry clusters make an attractive decoration in a small deciduous tree or on a garden wall. Do not confuse this pleasant, unarmed vine with greenbrier, *Smilax bona-nox,* which has similarly shaped leaves but is tough and spiny and produces dark blue-black berries in small inconspicuous clumps.

Anne Adams

Bois d'Arc, Bodark, Osage Orange
Maclura pomifera
Moraceae

Medium-sized thorny tree of variable shape with a distinct arc shape in its branches; produces large, knobby green fruit that turns yellow in the fall, usually near a stream.

LEAVES: Simple, alternate, deciduous; oval at base with a long point at tip; shiny, dense green, with distinct vein pattern on the upper surface.

FLOWERS: Small, green, male and female on different plants; April–June.

FRUIT: Huge, round, bumpy balls with a milky, acidic juice and seeds throughout; seeds mature in fall.

BARK: Thin, pale orange-brown when young, turning darker and thicker with deep furrows when mature.

RANGE: Central and northeastern Texas; southern corner of Oklahoma and Arkansas; occasionally in the Trans-Pecos, possibly planted by Native Americans; planted and naturalized across northern and eastern United States as living fences and hedgerows before invention of barbed wire.

Some Native American groups favored the arching branches of the bois d'arc for bow wood. The hard, heavy wood is resistant to decay and has been cut and used in the Hill Country for home construction piers. Its wood has also been made into fence posts and wagon-wheel hubs. The root bark produces a tan dye that was once used to obtain the khaki color of army uniforms. At one time, the city of Austin had streets paved with bois d'arc paving blocks. The large green fruit of this tree are eaten by horses and squirrels and are said to repel roaches.

Texas Mulberry
Morus microphylla
Moraceae

Shrub or small tree usually less than 15 feet tall; an occasional understory plant in canyons and near streams.

LEAVES: Simple, alternate, relatively small, about 2 inches long by nearly 1 inch wide; with toothed edges, rough on both sides, with a pointed tip.

FLOWERS: Small, greenish, in clusters, on short stalks; March–April.

FRUIT: In clusters on short stalks, whitish, red and then purple-black when ripe, edible; April–May.

BARK: Light gray, smooth with shallow furrows.

RANGE: Usually west of Colorado River in Texas; New Mexico, Arizona, and northern Mexico.

Texas mulberry is a desirable component of riparian undergrowth. Unfortunately, deer love its leaves and twigs and will browse it to death. When you find this plant, monitor its progress and, if necessary, place a wire cage around it to protect it from deer browse. Birds love its fruit so much that the fruit is rarely seen ripe. Native Americans of New Mexico and Arizona cultivated this plant for its fruit and for its elastic wood that was used to make bows.

Red Mulberry
Morus rubra
Moraceae

Can become a large tree, up to 40 feet tall, with a spreading crown; grows on creek and river bottoms and in moist woods.

LEAVES: Alternate, simple, deciduous, dull green; rough on top but softer below; edges with teeth but shape variable from pointy-tipped ovals to lobed or mittenlike.

FLOWERS: Inconspicuous, no petals, male and female on different plants; male flower spike 2–3 inches long, female about 1 inch long; appear with leaves in spring.

FRUIT: Edible, sweet but watery; shaped somewhat like a dewberry or blackberry; ripening from red to black in summer.

BARK: Dark gray-brown when mature, with large flakes.

RANGE: From Central Texas north to the Great Lakes, east to Massachusetts, and south to Florida.

Red mulberry can be confused with Carolina basswood or white mulberry, an import from China. Red mulberry fruit, scales on the twig buds, and milky sap from a broken twig will distinguish it from basswood. Red mulberry has red or blue fruit rather than white, and the lower surfaces of its leaves are covered with soft hairs. White mulberry (*M. alba*) has white to pinkish fruit, and the lower surfaces of its leaves are smooth except for small tufts of hairs on the largest veins.

Red mulberry is a desirable shade tree in the riparian zone along Texas Hill Country streams. When you see one in an undisturbed area, you will probably find others nearby. Birds and small mammals love the fruit. It is a host plant to mourning cloak butterflies. Red mulberry grows fast, is easy to transplant, and is relatively free of serious disease. When used as an ornamental, red mulberry will develop into an attractive tree if given adequate crown space.

Rufus Stephens

Elbow Bush, Spring Herald
Forestiera pubescens
Oleaceae

Irregular, straggling bush or sometimes a small tree to 15 feet tall;
common in thickets, open woods,
and fencerows and on good soil near
streams.

LEAVES: Simple, deciduous, medium-
sized, some almost diamond-
shaped; dull green above and
hairy below; opposite (as are the
branches).

FLOWERS: Yellow, very small, no
petals, easy to miss; male and
female on separate plants; first
flowers of the new year, before
the leaves; February–March.

FRUIT: Blue-black, small, fleshy,
with 1 seed; in pairs or clusters
along the new branches of female
plants; ripens in summer.

RANGE: Texas, west to California,
east to Florida, and north into
Oklahoma.

Though far from flashy, elbow bush
is easy to recognize by the downward
bow curve of its branches. Some even
have an elbowlike bend, thus the
common name. Elbow bush is a very
common component of Texas Hill
Country mixed brush and provides
important cover for many birds and
other wildlife. Its fruit is eaten by
birds and small mammals. The fruit
can be chewed with regular chewing
gum to create bubble gum.

Texas Ash
Fraxinus texensis
Oleaceae

A small tree growing to about 30 feet tall on rocky slopes, canyons, and bluffs that are usually protected from the west sun.

LEAVES: Pinnately compound, 5–8 inches long, usually with 5 leaflets (rarely 7); smooth on upper surface, edges smooth.

FLOWERS: Very small, purple, in small branching clusters; male and female separate; appear with the leaves; March.

FRUIT: About 1 inch long, single long wing off the end of each seed.

BARK: Light brown to gray, with irregular fissures; broken into plates with small, thin scales.

RANGE: Endemic to south-central Oklahoma and Central Texas.

Texas ash is so closely related to white ash, *F. americana,* that it may be a variety. Many species of birds and small mammals feed on the seeds, which are produced in abundance. Seedlings, which grow extremely slowly, are often found along Texas Hill Country streams. When a canopy opening is created by a dead or dying tree, Texas ash will sprint upward in the greater sunlight. It is a host plant to the tiger swallowtail butterfly.

INVASIVE EXOTIC SPECIES

Wax Leaf Ligustrum, Japanese Privet
Ligustrum japonicum
Oleaceae

Dark green, evergreen shrub or small tree with heavy, white flower clusters in summer; in moist settings, will grow in thick clumps.

LEAVES: Alternate, simple, leathery, shiny; up to 4 ½ inches long and 2 inches wide; upper surface dark green, lower surface lighter with obvious yellow central vein, edges smooth.

FLOWERS: White, ¼ inch wide, petals rolled back; in dense clusters up to 8 inches long, at ends of small branches.

FRUIT: Blue-black, round, about ¼ inch wide, in large clusters; hangs on into winter.

TWIGS: At first, green or gray-brown and smooth; later, with small corky bumps that start out round and turn into horizontal slits on older branches.

RANGE: From Japan and Asia; invaded southeastern United States from Texas east to Florida and Maryland.

Wax leaf ligustrum is a common ornamental shrub used throughout Texas and other Southern states. Its popularity stems from its rapid growth, hefty size, durability, attractive flowers, and evergreen foliage. It seems to be a perfect shrub for any yard, but wax leaf ligustrum has a major drawback. It escapes cultivation, spreads into natural settings, and displaces native species. Wherever wax leaf ligustrum grows in the wild, it should be removed. The riparian management section of this book gives control methods.

Bracted Passion Flower
Passiflora affinis
Passifloraceae

Climbs on shrubs and small trees and is found in a variety of environments, including creek bottoms and high, rocky ravines.

LEAVES: Smooth, 3-lobed, 1 ½–5 inches wide and 1–4 inches long; deeply lobed with tiny yellowish spots that probably mimic butterfly eggs and discourage egg laying.

FLOWERS: Typical intricate passion flower structure but pale yellow-green and small, about 1 inch in diameter, filaments purplish near base, tiny dark bracts on stems; May–September.

FRUIT: Small, almost round, green, capsulelike berry turning purple-black when ripe.

RANGE: Edwards Plateau.

Look for this vine in the summer and early fall when you might get lucky and spot one of its intricate flowers. It is a beautiful but unobtrusive vine that hosts some spectacular butterflies, including the orange-and-black gulf fritillary and yellow-and-black zebra longwing.

Another passion-flower, not pictured here, corona de Cristo (*P. foetida* var. *gossypifolia*) is also found in the Texas Hill Country. It has pale pinkish flowers 1–2 inches in diameter and bright red seed pods.

Spreadlobe Passion Flower
Passiflora tenuiloba
Passifloraceae

A vine that can be hidden right before your eyes—low in a tangle of vines and shrubs or along a fence line—with small flowers and leaves shaped like miniature airplanes.

LEAVES: Variable, each with 3 basic lobes forming a T with the top of the T much wider than the base; lateral lobes about 2–4 inches wide, central lobe about 1–2 inches long; small pair of glands at base of each leaf.

FLOWERS: Intricate, about ¾ inch wide, pale yellow-green with a touch of maroon; May–October.

FRUIT: Small, green at first, black when ripe.

RANGE: Texas and New Mexico.

Look carefully for this small vine. The plant in the photograph climbs on greenbrier in a mix of vines and brush growing in dry caliche. With *P. tenuiloba,* big is not better. Its blossoms are small but amazingly intricate, and its leaves are small but unlike any other leaf you will ever see. If its foliage appears to have been chewed, look for the yellow-and-black zebra longwing or gulf fritillary caterpillars that might be living on them.

John Millsaps

American Sycamore, Plane Tree
Platanus occidentalis
Platanaceae

Tree found along streams and in bottomlands; most striking feature is the exceptionally smooth, white and light brown trunk.

LEAVES: Large, wide, simple, alternate, deciduous; with 3–5 pointed lobes; bright green above and paler and hairy below.

FLOWERS: Male and female on same tree but in separate, tight, round clusters at the end of a short stalk; April–May.

FRUIT: In the fall, dark brown balls at end of a stalk 3–6 inches long; holding small seeds that hang on and are obvious through much of the winter.

BARK: Greenish brown at first, scaling off in thin pieces to expose pale white younger bark.

RANGE: Throughout eastern and central United States; north to Ontario, Canada, south to Florida, and west to Texas.

Young sycamore trees spring up and grow like weeds on rocky or gravelly bottomland, where they are the first tree to become established in areas scoured by erosion. They can grow to great heights and provide light shade. This tree is a favorite with children for climbing because of the comfortable smooth trunk and large branches. Although it warps easily and is difficult to work, sycamore wood has been used in many ways, such as in crates and butcher blocks. First cultivated as a shade tree in 1640, the sycamore is easy to start from seeds.

Old Man's Beard
Clematis drummondii
Ranunculaceae

Climbing vine common on fences and plants in dry soils; very obvious when it goes to seed in late summer and fall, making long white "beards."

LEAVES: Opposite, compound, with 5–7 leaflets, ½–1 inch long, often 3-lobed; petioles long, slender, and twisted, giving plant a way to climb.

FLOWERS: Yellow-white, about ¾ inch in diameter; no petals, sepals look like petals.

FRUIT: Small, dry seeds with long, silky white hairs; conspicuous late July–October.

RANGE: Central, South, and West Texas; New Mexico, Arizona, and northern Mexico.

Clematis is a genus that includes about 250 species, 13 that grow in Texas but only 3 in the Hill Country. Of the Hill Country species, old man's beard is the most common and conspicuous. For information about the other two, see *Wildflowers of the Texas Hill Country* by Marshall Enquist.

The species is named for Thomas Drummond, a botanist from Scotland, who collected and studied plants in Texas during 1833–35. He became so fond of Texas that he planned to bring his family here, but he died collecting plants in Cuba on his way back to Scotland.

Old man's beard is a host plant to the fatal metalmark butterfly. Deer browse its leaves. This vine is woody only near the base.

Redroot
Ceanothus herbaceus
Rhamnaceae

A low, spreading shrub with delicate white spring flower clusters; found on rocky road banks, in shady cedar-oak woodlands, and in stony open fields.

LEAVES: Simple, alternate, deciduous, about 1 inch long; in shape of narrow, somewhat pointed ovals, with fine teeth on the margins and prominent pale veins on the lower surfaces.

FLOWERS: Small, white; in dense, rounded clusters usually at the end of a branch; March–May.

FRUIT: Many round, 3-celled capsules, black when mature; September–November.

RANGE: Central Texas, north to South Dakota and Minnesota, and east to Quebec and Florida.

Redroot may not appear to be a real shrub because only the lower parts are woody. It is included in wildflower books because of its attractive spring blossoms. Two species of redroot grow in the Hill Country. *C. americanus* is very similar to *C. herbaceus,* but the leaves are a little wider. The leaves of both species were used as substitute for tea during the Civil War. Their roots make huge globs close to the surface, called "grubs" because they had to be "grubbed" out before a field could be plowed. The common name derives from the fact that red dye can be extracted from the roots. In some areas, redroot is considered good browse for livestock. Birds, including bobwhite quail, feed on the seeds. It is a host plant to the azure blue butterfly.

Hog Plum, Texas Snakewood
Colubrina texensis
Rhamnaceae

A sturdy, low, dense, spreading, thornless shrub of shallow rocky soil.

LEAVES: Deciduous, ½–1 inch long; sometimes hairy and sometimes smooth; edges with fine teeth, parallel veins.

FLOWERS: Small, alternate, greenish with an unusual starlike shape; April–May.

FRUIT: Dark outer husk, small, round, pink-tan; with 3 chambers and 3 shiny, brown seeds that hang on plant for a long time.

TWIGS: Pale gray, zigzag, short, stiff.

RANGE: Edwards Plateau, Rio Grande Plains, coastal plains, the Trans-Pecos.

Hog plum is found in many different situations. It prefers well-drained soil and will invade heavily disturbed land. Hog plum is poisonous to sheep but is browsed by deer, and its fruit is eaten by birds, small mammals, and javelinas. The genus name *Colubrina* means "serpent," and the zigzag twigs have the look of a little snake.

Steve Nelle

Green Condalia
Condalia viridis
Rhamnaceae

A locally abundant, spreading, medium to large, thorny shrub.

LEAVES: Bright green, young leaves have a few small hairs and later become smooth; small, wider than long, a little wider beyond the middle.

FLOWERS: Tiny, solitary or paired between leaf and stem; no petals.

FRUIT: Small black fruit with single seed.

TWIGS: Gray young twigs have bristles and old ones are smooth.

RANGE: From western Bandera, Kerr, and Gillespie Counties westward through Big Bend; also in Chihuahua, Mexico.

Condalia viridis can be common in dry uplands, along gravel washes and dry stream beds. It is one of five or more spiny shrubs in this genus that occur in West and South Texas. Green condalia produces berries eaten by birds. Because of its densely armored character, green condalia serves as excellent protected cover for birds' nests and as a nursery plant for other plants susceptible to deer browse. Green condalia wood (heartwood) is a beautiful burnt orange color and is so dense that it sinks in water.

Bill Ward

Carolina Buckthorn
Frangula caroliniana
(Rhamnus caroliniana)
Rhamnaceae

Small tree with a slender trunk, lustrous green leaves, and abundant, long-lasting, yellow, red, and black berries; found in fencerows and thickets, at the top of ravines, and near streams.

LEAVES: Simple, alternate, 2–5 inches long; very smooth, shiny, dark green with distinct veins; more pointed at the tip than at the base; deciduous late in the fall.

FLOWERS: Small, yellow-white, single or in clusters growing from the base of leaves; late spring–early summer.

FRUIT: Round, sweet; yellow, red, and finally black when mature; late summer–fall.

BARK: Gray, thin, smooth, with shallow furrows.

RANGE: From Edwards Plateau east to Florida and north to Missouri.

Carolina buckthorn is a handsome small tree, tolerant of shade or sun. It has beautiful summer foliage and bright fall color. Because this tree is good browse for white-tailed deer, it is often seen growing within the protection of a spiny shrub such as agarita. Carolina buckthorn is a host plant to gray hairstreak, spring azure, and painted lady butterflies, and its abundant fruit provides food for several species of birds.

Bill Ward

Coyotillo
Karwinskia humboldtiana
Rhamnaceae

Attractive, thornless shrub or small tree growing in shallow, dry soil on far southern edge of Edwards Plateau.

LEAVES: Shiny, dark green, 1–2 inches long, opposite, with entire margins, firm and with strong veins.

FLOWERS: Inconspicuous, greenish; summer and fall

FRUIT: Small, brown or black.

BARK: Smooth, gray to red-brown.

RANGE: Central America, Mexico, and South Texas Plains north onto the southern edge of Edwards Plateau and abundant on Rio Grande Plains and southern parts of the Trans-Pecos.

Coyotillo in the wild is usually 2 to 6 feet tall but can grow into a small tree up to about 20 feet tall. It is an attractive plant with striking, evergreen leaves and could be an excellent xeric landscape shrub or small tree. Coyotillo is easily propagated by root divi-

sions and can be trimmed into a good hedge. At the same time, it is important to know that coyotillo leaves and especially the berries contain a neurotoxin dangerous to humans and domestic animals, including cattle, sheep, goats, hogs, and chickens. Symptoms include weakness, lack of coordination, paralysis, prostration, and death. As with most toxic plants, animals do not consume it if there are other desirable plants available. Coyotes and wild birds are reported to be able to digest it without ill effect. In Mexico, coyotillo has many local common names.

Susan M. Sander

INVASIVE EXOTIC SPECIES

Jujube
Ziziphus zizyphus (Z. jujuba)
Rhamnaceae

A deciduous small tree with stout thorns, dark foliage, and cherry- or plum-sized edible fruit in summer; spreads into the wild around older trees in the Hill Country.

LEAVES: Shiny, with shallow scalloped edges, on zigzag branches.

FLOWERS: Single or in small clusters at base of leaves; May.

FRUIT: Turns from green to brown, fleshy with bland flavor.

RANGE: From China; has escaped into the wild in Texas, Utah, Louisiana, Alabama, Georgia, and northern Florida.

Jujube is tolerant of alkaline soil, is nearly disease free, and spreads by root sprouts and seed. It is related to lotebush, *Z. obtusifolia,* a deciduous, thorny native shrub that often grows with mesquite and prickly pear in South Texas.

Michael Margo

Mountain Mahogany
Cercocarpus montanus
Rosaceae
Shrub or small tree on dry, rocky, upland slopes of western Edwards Plateau.

LEAVES: Simple, alternate, oval or egg-shaped, about 1 inch long, gray-green; margin usually with teeth near the tip, leathery with leaf veins prominent on lower surface.

FLOWERS: Small, white-yellowish, single or in clusters of 3, March–June.

FRUIT: Small, brown, leathery fruit each tipped with 1–3 inch long hairy awns.

TWIGS: Stout, rigid, and rough from leaf scars.

RANGE: Occurs in limited locations in Trans-Pecos and Edwards Plateau east to Junction. Also, occasional in Oregon, Baja California, Utah, South Dakota, New Mexico, and the Texas and Oklahoma panhandles.

Mountain mahogany wood is very hard and dark. Native Americans used it to make digging sticks and knife handles and as a distaff when spinning wool. Mountain mahogany is a small rugged tree that is highly drought, heat, and fire tolerant. After a fire, their tops may be killed but they sprout new growth from the root crown and return quickly. Mountain mahogany conserves water by dropping its leaves during hot, dry seasons. Healthy stands often cover a large, continuous area. It has plumed fruit that are much more attractive than the flowers.

Emilie Rogers

Hawthorn
Crataegus sp.
Rosaceae

Infrequent, small trees or large
shrubs, 5–16 feet tall, with long, sharp
thorns; usually grows in bottomland
soil near an intermittent water source
but also in fencerows and in heavy
mixed deciduous shrubs and vines
where it gets protection from deer
browse.

Emilie Rogers

LEAVES: Shiny, dark green,
    ¾–1 ½ inches long, toothed, with
    parallel veins.
FLOWERS: Flat-topped clusters,
    ½–¾ inch wide; 5 white petals;
    appear briefly in mid-April.
FRUIT: Round and fleshy, like a rose-
    hip with remnant of flower
    on its outer end, in clusters.
RANGE: Central Texas.

The taxonomy of the Hill Country
Crataegus is uncertain, and there may
be several species that are very hard

to separate, so all can be conveniently
treated as one. These are attractive woody plants worth knowing
and protecting. Unless growing in a
thicket or wire cage, young hawthorn
plants are browsed to death by deer.
Hawthorn is a host plant to gray hairstreak, banded hairstreak, tiger swallowtail, viceroy, and red-spotted
admiral butterflies.

Blanco Crabapple
Malus ioënsis var. *texensis*
(Pyrus ioënsis var. *texana)*
Rosaceae

A small tree with an open, rounded crown and beautiful pink and white spring blossoms; found only in limited areas of Blanco, Kerr, and Kendall counties and nearly always within the protection of a "nurse" plant.

LEAVES: Simple, deciduous, usually 2–3 inches long; alternate or on short spur shoots, oval, teeth on edges, some with shallow lobes; upper surface green and fairly smooth, lower surface covered with dense, white hairs.

FLOWERS: Pink buds opening into pale pink flowers with 5 petals; appear with or before leaves in April.

FRUIT: Small, bitter green apples; ripen in October.

BARK: Dark gray with long, vertical ridges about ¼ inch thick when mature.

Blanco crabapple is well suited to the Hill Country's hot climate but is heavily browsed by white-tailed deer. The tremendous increase in deer populations (following the eradication of the screwworm fly that often killed newborn fawns) now threatens the growth of new Blanco crabapple trees in the wild. Some local nurseries sell this lovely but slow-growing tree, which is well suited to landscape use as long as it is protected from deer. Early Texas pioneers used the apples for homemade jelly. They require a lot of sugar, and the flavor can be enhanced by removing a thick, greasy covering on the skin with washings of hot water.

Texas Almond
Prunus minutiflora
Rosaceae

Low, thicket-forming shrub on dry slopes in shallow soils over limestone.

LEAVES: Simple, alternate; very small, usually less than ¾ inch long, leathery; oval shape with round or sometimes pointed tip and tapered base.

FLOWERS: Less than ¼ inch long, cream-colored, fragile, in tight clusters; February–March.

FRUIT: Less than ½ inch long, flattened, fine hair, large stone, little flesh.

RANGE: Texas from Colorado River to beyond the Pecos River; Chihuahua, Mexico.

Texas almond is often overlooked because of its nondescript character. Check the bark carefully to see its silver and gray bands. New growth will have dense, woolly hairs on the twigs. This is an important habitat plant that provides shelter and food for small mammals and birds.

Creek Plum
Prunus rivularis
Rosaceae

Slender shrubs usually growing in clumps along creek bottoms and fencerows; best identified in early spring by numerous, eye-catching, fragrant white blossoms.

LEAVES: Simple, deciduous, alternate or clustered on short spurs, up to 2 ½ inches long; slender, smooth, shiny, with serrate edges; emerge with or after blossoms.

FLOWERS: White or cream, 5 petals, about 1 ½ inches wide; arise in clusters along upper stems; February–March.

FRUIT: Yellow to bright red, fleshy, up to ¾ inch in diameter, with an oblong stone; ripens June–September.

RANGE: Central Texas and Oklahoma. Fairly common in its limited range, creek plum goes unnoticed except in early spring when its abundant white blossoms are remarkable against the drab brown landscape. Individual plants are usually less than 6 feet tall, and creek plums form attractive thickets that provide good cover for a variety of birds. Fruit is small and tart and eaten by birds and small mammals.

A few local native plant growers now sell creek plum. There is also a similar but less common species, Mexican plum (*P. mexicana*). This plant is a small tree with somewhat larger leaves, blossoms, and fruit. It does not form thickets and is more common in local nurseries.

Escarpment Black Cherry, Black Cherry
Prunus serotina var. *eximia*
Rosaceae

Locally common and attractive medium-sized tree; grows on hillsides, canyons, and creek bottoms of the Edwards Plateau.

LEAVES: Simple, deciduous, shiny, 3–5 inches long; dark green, pale on the lower surface, with tiny teeth along the edges; turn bright yellow in November.

FLOWERS: Small, white, with 5 tiny petals on slender stalks 4–6 inches long that hang among the outer leaves; March–April.

FRUIT: Round, purple, ¼–⅜ inch, thin flesh, single center stone; late summer.

BARK: Silver and gray bands on young stems and branches; older bark dark gray-silver, rough.

RANGE: Limited to Edwards Plateau and south-central Texas.

Black cherry grows naturally with bigtooth maple, cedar elm, Spanish oak, and flameleaf sumac, creating brilliant yellow, orange, and red fall landscapes. It is a component of the Texas Hill Country hardwood mix that appears to be in decline. In many places, deer consume most or all seedlings, preventing regeneration. Black cherry provides food and shelter for birds and small mammals and is a host plant to banded hairstreak, spring azure, eastern tiger swallowtail, two-tailed tiger swallowtail, painted lady, viceroy, and red-spotted admiral butterflies. Lovely white spring blossoms, bright yellow fall color, attractive shape, and rapid growth rate make this a perfect yard tree for poor soil conditions with some protection from the west sun.

INVASIVE EXOTIC SPECIES

Pyracantha, Firethorn
Pyracantha koidzumii
Rosaceae

A large, gangly, thorny, evergreen bush with bright red fall berries.

LEAVES: Simple, slender, ¾–1 ½ inches long, leathery; smooth edges, tips rounded; most in clusters at tips of very short branches.

FLOWERS: White, with 5 petals, in fairly tight clusters; April–May.

FRUIT: Less than ½ inch wide, red, numerous; often present in winter.

RANGE: Native to Taiwan; widely cultivated and escaped into the wild in numerous places.

Pyracantha's beautiful red berries make it popular with gardeners and birds. Unfortunately, the birds have spread the seeds of this plant, so it is now found invading pastures, woodlands, and fencerows throughout the Texas Hill Country and beyond.

Dewberry, Zarzamora
Rubus riograndis
Rosaceae

A trailing, prickly shrub, commonly forming dense patches in fields, along roadsides, and in thickets.

LEAVES: Alternate, compound; 3–5 leaflets, each leaflet a narrow oval with coarse teeth on the margins.

FLOWERS: White, with 5 petals, up to 1 inch wide; March–April.

FRUIT: Delicious berry, black when ripe; small (¼–½ inch) when rain is inadequate but large (more than 1 inch long), sweet, and juicy during years with good rainfall; matures in June.

RANGE: From Texas and Oklahoma east to Maryland and Florida.

Dewberries provide important food and shelter for many types of wildlife, including box turtles and small mammals. In years when dewberries are plump and plentiful, they are delicious on breakfast cereal and make good pies and cobblers.

Common Buttonbush
Cephalanthus occidentalis
Rubiaceae

Loose, branching shrub commonly found in wet soil of streams and ponds; easily recognized by the round, white, ball-shaped flower heads present all summer.

LEAVES: Deciduous, simple, 3–6 inches long; opposite or in a whorl of 3; oval-shaped with long point at tip, no teeth; shiny green upper surface and duller below.

FLOWERS: Small, round, with long yellow stamens in a dense, white, ball-shaped cluster; June–September.

FRUIT: Compact, rough, brown balls approximately 1 inch in diameter.

RANGE: In or near water throughout southern Canada and most of the United States.

Buttonbush is a handsome ornamental shrub for wet, poorly drained soils. Its aromatic blossoms produce nectar for butterflies and bees. Ducks and other waterbirds eat the seeds and nest in its branches. Buttonbush leaves usually are not eaten by deer or livestock. Butterflies, especially skippers, swallowtails, and hairstreaks, love the nectar of buttonbush.

Wafer Ash, Hop Tree
Ptelea trifoliata
Rutaceae

Multitrunked shrub or small tree growing in fencerows, near streams, and in shaded woodlands.

LEAVES: Opposite or alternate, compound; 3 medium-sized leaflets attached at base; strong smell when crushed.

FLOWERS: Yellow-green, 4–5 petals, in clusters with new leaves, sweet-smelling; April.

FRUIT: In round, flat, paperlike wings that are first green and then dry to tan; each almost 1 inch wide, in clusters; distinctive in late summer and fall.

RANGE: Across the United States and into parts of eastern Canada.

Walking past a wafer ash in bloom, you will probably smell the flowers before seeing them. Early spring flowers are more fragrant than eye-catching and produce clusters of flat, round, winged seeds. Early settlers used its fruit instead of true hops to make beer. Its bark and roots also have been used as a substitute for quinine in the treatment of malaria. Today, some local growers offer this plant as an attractive shrub that provides dependable fall color for shaded locations. Wafer ash is a host plant to eastern tiger swallowtail, two-tailed swallowtail, and giant swallowtail butterflies. Deer rarely bother this shrub.

Tickle Tongue, Toothachetree, Lime Prickly Ash
Zanthoxylum hirsutum
Rutaceae

Aromatic and thorny shrub or, rarely, a small tree with shiny compound leaves that have a pungent citrus smell when crushed; found in both calcareous and sandy soils along fencerows and woodland edges.

LEAVES: Compound with small thorns, 3–7 glossy leaflets with crinkled, toothed edges.

FLOWERS: Greenish, in clusters; early spring.

FRUIT: Round, ¼ inch, red-brown capsule.

RANGE: Arkansas, Oklahoma, and Texas.

Although ranchers do not like this shrub because it is not browsed by livestock or deer, tickle tongue fruit and seeds are good bird food. Its thorny branches provide excellent cover and nest sites for birds. Tickle tongue is a host plant for the giant swallowtail butterfly.

When chewed, its leaves will numb your mouth; they are especially strong in spring and summer. If you hold a leaf up to the light, you will see that the leaf is dotted with tiny holes. The mouth-numbing substance comes from these holes.

Cottonwood
Populus deltoides
Salicaceae

A grand, airy tree with leaves that quake and rattle in the breeze; often grows high (up to 100 feet tall) above the other trees along a waterway.

LEAVES: Simple, alternate, deciduous, 3–7 inches long, smooth; triangular with an elongated tip and scalloped margins; shiny green above and veins obvious on lower surface.

FLOWERS: Male and female catkins on separate trees; male catkins about 2 inches long; female catkins up to 4 inches long; March–May.

FRUIT: Small capsules with many seeds in each pod, each seed with a long tuft of "cotton" that allows it to be carried by the wind; seeds ripen May–June.

BARK: Smooth, thin, yellow-gray on young trees; darker gray with deep furrows and distinct flat-topped ridges on mature trees.

RANGE: Widespread northeastern tree with many varieties growing from Rocky Mountains to the east coast and Canada to Texas.

Cottonwood is an excellent tree for restoring a riparian habitat. As a pioneer plant, it grows up to 5 feet per year in the first twenty-five years, has widespread shallow roots, and will re-seed itself. Its loose crown has many branches that may bend down over the stream but are usually high and upright on the trunk. Cottonwood trees do not bear fruit or "cotton" until they are about ten years old. When they do not get the high amount of water they need, cottonwood trees are prone to many pests and fungal diseases. Cottonwood is a host plant for eastern tiger swallowtail, viceroy, mourning cloak, and red-spotted admiral butterflies. Its leaves, bark, and seeds are eaten by wildlife. Rose-breasted grosbeaks are especially fond of cottonwood seeds. In other areas, trees of this genus are used to produce pulp for paper and wood for crates, plywood, veneer, and musical instruments. The state champion cottonwood tree grows in Bandera County and is 80 feet tall with a trunk circumference of 372 inches.

Anne Adams

Black Willow
Salix nigra
Salicaceae

Fast-growing, narrow-leafed tree, often with several trunks; found growing in wet soil along streams and ponds.

LEAVES: Simple, alternate, deciduous; long, narrow, with very fine-toothed edges and a highly tapered tip; turn yellow in fall.

FLOWERS: On elongated clusters 1–2 inches long; male and female on separate plants; appear with new leaves; April–May.

FRUIT: Minute seeds held in ¼-inch, green-pale yellow capsules; windborne on bright white, silky hairs; seeds mature in late spring and early summer.

BARK: Brown to black, rough with deep ridges, becoming shaggy with age.

RANGE: Across eastern two-thirds of Texas, east to the Carolinas, and north to New Brunswick and North Dakota.

The black willow averages 4 feet of growth per year. Its wood is weak and its life span short. The willow's extensive shallow roots make it useful in erosion control. Willow branches have been used as divining rods to locate water. Native Americans made an infusion of the bark to lower fever and reduce aches and pains. European settlers made baby teething necklaces from the young twigs and also used twig ends to clean their teeth. Willow bark contains salicin, which once was used in the production of aspirin; today, aspirin is manufactured synthetically.

Black willow is a host plant for eastern tiger swallowtail, viceroy, mourning cloak, and red-spotted admiral butterflies. It often grows on banks of ponds where a large tangle of roots provides protection for minnows, small fish, and aquatic invertebrates. Mature black willow near water also serves as a favorite roost and perch site for heron, egrets, and kingfishers.

Western Soapberry, Jaboncillo
Sapindus saponaria var. *drummondii*
Sapindaceae

A small or medium-sized tree with large, eye-catching cream-colored flower clusters in late spring and early summer; found throughout Texas along fencerows, near streams, and on woodland edges.

LEAVES: Deciduous, alternate, pinnately compound, up to 1 ½ feet long; usually 4–19 long, narrow leaflets that appear to be in even pairs, often no terminal leaflet; dull yellow-green turning bright yellow in early fall.

FLOWERS: Small, cream-colored in large clusters, 6–10 inches long; April–June.

FRUIT: Smooth, round balls, ½ inch in diameter; nearly transparent, darken with age; dry to hard and wrinkled, in loose branched clusters; mature in fall and often remain attached until next spring.

BARK: Rough, flaky, gray to pale reddish tan.

RANGE: Kansas and Missouri south to northern Mexico; Colorado and Arizona east to Louisiana.

Its slender shape and long, narrow, compound leaves give this common but often overlooked tree a light, airy look. Western soapberry has been a popular ornamental tree for many years throughout its range. It is disease resistant, tolerates poor soil, has a moderate growth rate, and produces handsome fall color. It has been called "wild china tree" because its fruit resembles those of the chinaberry tree.

The fruit of the western soapberry contains the alkaloid saponin, which produces a good lather and is still used for washing clothes in Mexico. Although irritating to some people's skin, the fruits are made into attractive buttons, necklaces, and rosaries and have medicinal properties used to lower fever and treat kidney disorders. The wood splits easily and has been used to make baskets and saddlepack frames. The leaves may be poisonous. Western soapberry is host to the soapberry hairstreak butterfly.

Mexican Buckeye
Ungnadia speciosa
Sapindaceae

A large branching shrub with bright pink blossoms that stand out in spring and large, 3-chambered, woody seed pods distinctive throughout the year; found all over the Texas Hill Country in canyons and on creek banks.

LEAVES: Deciduous, alternate, compound, up to 1 foot long; 5–7 leaflets in pairs with 1 at tip end; shiny dark green above, turning bright yellow in fall.

FLOWERS: Showy, bright pink, in clusters crowded along twigs before or with new spring leaves; March–April.

FRUIT: Glossy, dark brown seeds, each with a pale spot; seeds mature in fall within thin, 3-chambered shell that splits open from below.

RANGE: Central Texas west to southern New Mexico and south into northeastern Mexico.

The common name comes from the shiny, brown seeds, but this plant is not a member of the true buckeye family. Children like to carry and play with the large seeds, which are easy to germinate. Although considered poisonous, the seeds can pass through a human digestive tract without causing harm. The blossoms, which attract butterflies and honeybees, appear at the same time as, and from a distance resemble, those of the Texas redbud. Most deer do not eat this shrub. It is a host plant to the Henry's elfin butterfly.

Gum Bumelia, Coma
Sideroxylon lanuginosum
(Bumelia lanuginosa)
Sapotaceae

Usually encountered as a nondescript shrub or small tree with short, stout branchlets that sometimes have a thorn at the tip.

LEAVES: Simple, alternate or in clusters, slender, up to 2 ½ inches long but usually smaller; smooth above and hairy below; edges smooth and down-curved, base more tapering than the tip end.

FLOWERS: Inconspicuous, white, with pungent scent; in small clusters growing from the base of the leaves; June–July.

FRUIT: Small, black, oval berry made mostly of a single brown seed; ripens September–October.

BARK: Brown, fairly thick, making a pattern of narrow, flat-topped ridges.

Gum bumelia is occasionally mistaken for a small live oak. It is easily overlooked growing in fencerows and thickets, on dry uplands, and along streams. Deer often rub the velvet off their antlers on this small, sturdy tree. Its flowers attract a metallic green beetle. Gum bumelia is a root sprouter and sometimes forms thickets that provide good nest sites for many birds. Birds and small mammals love the fruit, but it can cause stomach upset in humans. Gum bumelia got its name because children used to chew the gum that forms at wounds on the trunk or branches.

Cenizo, Purple Sage
Leucophyllum frutescens
Scrophulariaceae

A popular ornamental gray bush with violet or pink blossoms, native and common on limestone soil in South Texas plains; found naturally in a few places, such as Barton Springs, on the eastern and southern edges of the Hill Country.

LEAVES: Alternate or clustered, evergreen; soft, silver gray to light gray-green; small ovals usually attached directly to stem.

FLOWERS: Lavender-pink, nearly bell-shaped, about ¾ inch long and wide; intermittent spring–fall.

FRUIT: Small capsule with many seeds.

RANGE: Trans-Pecos, southern edge of the Texas Hill Country, South Texas, and Mexico.

Cenizo is a popular ranch-gate planting and is used extensively in highway as well as home landscaping. It does well on poor but well-drained soil. Deer occasionally will browse the leaves. Blossoms often appear following late spring rains and again after early fall rain. They attract many butterflies and bees. Cenizo is a host plant to Theona checkerspot butterfly.

Snapdragon Vine
Maurandya antirrhiniflora
Scrophulariaceae

Low-growing, twining vine 3–10 feet long; inhabits rocky, limestone soil and grows in masses over other plants, vines, and fences through southern half of the Texas Hill Country.

LEAVES: Triangular, arrow-shaped, ½–1 inch long, light green; surfaces without hairs, edges smooth.

FLOWERS: Petals joined into a tube shape, purple–dark blue with white or cream-colored center; March–September.

FRUIT: Round capsule, ¼ inch wide.

RANGE: Central and South Texas and the Trans-Pecos.

Snapdragon vine is an herbaceous vine included here because it is often discounted and cleared with brush removal. It forms masses when it grows in good conditions, thus creating excellent habitat for insects and lizards, which are important animals on the lower end of food chains that support many other creatures. Snapdragon vine has delicate beauty that makes it a good landscape plant. It prefers well-drained soil, regular water, sun with some shade from afternoon sun, and protection from the north winter wind.

Sycamore Leaf Snowbell
Styrax platanifolius
Styracaceae

A sprawling irregular shrub that grows on steep banks and bluffs near water; conspicuous in spring when it has spectacular white blossoms and in the fall when it has bright yellow leaves.

LEAVES: Large, simple, alternate, deciduous; nearly round with dull points suggesting the shape of a sycamore leaf.

FLOWERS: Exceptionally beautiful, large, white bells with yellow stamens; hang down from branches under the leaves; April–May.

FRUIT: Small, pale, round capsule with a short tip; matures in fall.

RANGE: Only on Edwards Plateau of Central Texas.

The sycamore leaf snowbell is one of the Hill Country's most beautiful and uncommon shrubs. Look for small, sycamore-type leaves on a large bush growing in the shade near the top of steep places along a creek or drainage. When you find one in a good location, you are likely to discover more in the same locality. Not only are the spring blossoms a rare treat but in the fall snowbell leaves turn bright yellow (sometimes with large brown dots made by a fungus) and stand out remarkably against their dull surroundings. Late fall is a good time of year to find and identify plants growing in their rough and often crowded terrain. It is a host plant to the tiger swallowtail butterfly.

The endangered species *S. texanus* is a close relative and very similar to *S. platanifolius*. *S. texanus* grows only in highly restricted sites in Edwards and Real counties.

Linden, Carolina Basswood
Tilia americana var. *caroliniana (T. caroliniana)*
Tiliaceae

Large tree sometimes mistaken for red mulberry; found scattered in fertile soil along streams and valleys.

LEAVES: Large, simple, alternate, deciduous; somewhat heart-shaped but with an uneven base; upper surface dark green, lower surface lighter and covered with rust-colored hairs.

FLOWERS: Small, cream-colored, fragrant; in a cluster growing from a distinctive long, narrow bract; late spring and early summer.

FRUIT: Woolly, round, pea-sized; encloses 1–2 hard seeds; hangs in clusters from the leafy bract as do the flowers; matures in fall.

BARK: Gray, smooth on young plants; later, develops flat-topped, interlacing ridges with shallow, irregular grooves.

RANGE: From Central Texas north into Arkansas and east to the Carolinas and northern Florida.

Linden, also commonly called basswood, may be confused with the more common red mulberry. Identify it by the lopsided base of its leaves and the unique leaflike bract from which the flowers and seed clusters grow. Also, its winter buds have two to four scales; those of the red mulberry have at least five. Some trees have multiple trunks suckering from the base of the main trunk. American basswood, a northern relative, is a popular ornamental tree, but the Hill Country species is not yet readily available in nurseries. All basswoods have light, straight-grained wood that is easy to work. Because it does not warp or check readily, it was commonly used for furniture and is good for whittling. Flowers and leaves have been used to treat colds, coughs, and sore throats. The gummy inner bark soothes minor burns and skin irritations. Linden flowers produce nectar that makes honey. It is a host plant for the eastern comma, mourning cloak, white M hairstreak, and red-spotted admiral butterflies.

Netleaf Hackberry, Palo Blanco
Celtis laevigata var. *reticulata*
Ulmaceae

A medium-sized tree recognized by prominent warts on light gray bark, rough lance-shaped leaves, and small red "hackberries" during late summer and fall; common in thickets and woodlands on rocky or bottomland soil.

LEAVES: Alternate, simple, deciduous, usually 2–4 inches long; oval with a long, tapering tip; both surfaces with prominent veins; base often tapered on one side and rounded on the other.

FLOWERS: Inconspicuous, green; spring.

FRUIT: Small, dull red, sweet, round, with a large single stone; ripens early fall.

BARK: Light gray, thin, easily damaged, with corky warts that produce a rough appearance.

RANGE: From Central Texas north to Missouri, east to Virginia, and south to Florida.

Many people consider hackberry a "trash" tree, but hackberry is an integral component of many natural thickets that are essential wildlife habitat. It often has mistletoe on its branches and is common in vacant lots and fencerows. These wild thickets also form useful sound barriers and privacy screens for rural and suburban residents. Hackberry fruit contain fats that are a primary source of energy for migrant birds. The fruit is also popular with resident birds and small mammals. Hackberries are host plants for American snout, emperor, and question mark butterflies.

Sugarberry or sugar hackberry, *C. laevigata* var. *laevigata,* is another common Texas Hill Country hackberry. It is very similar to net leaf hackberry; however, the two trees are easy to distinguish because sugarberry has somewhat narrower leaves that are smooth and have a sweet taste in the spring. Central Texas is on the western edge of sugarberry range and the eastern edge of netleaf hackberry range.

Cedar Elm
Ulmus crassifolia
Ulmaceae

Common, xeric, slender trees, usually with buttressed trunks, graceful branches, and typically narrow crowns.

LEAVES: Simple, deciduous, alternate; small, 1–2 inches long; stiff, rough on top with serrate edges; often turn yellow in fall.

FLOWERS: Inconspicuous blossoms in clusters at the base of a leaf; only native elm species to flower in late summer or fall rather than spring.

FRUIT: Surrounded by a round, flat wing, ¼–½ inch in diameter; often abundant and eye-catching in pale tan clusters; single seeds mature in fall.

BARK: Paired, parallel corky ridges or wings on many young branches and seedlings.

RANGE: From Central Texas and Arkansas east to Mississippi.

The species name *crassifolia* means "thick leaf." This is by far the most common of the Hill Country elms and is easily recognized by its elegant upright shape and small leaves that turn yellow in the fall. A tough, popular Hill Country shade tree, cedar elm grows in many soil types, is drought tolerant, is easily transplanted, and can withstand heavy seasonal flooding. It becomes especially large and full in bottomland. One giant cedar elm grows in a seasonal creek that runs through Fair Oaks Ranch Homeowners Park in northern Bexar County. This tree has such a large, wide crown that from a distance it can be mistaken for an American or slippery elm.

The seeds of the cedar elm are eaten by turkeys and small mammals. Cedar elms are host plants for question mark, comma, mourning cloak, and painted lady butterflies.

Slippery Elm
Ulmus rubra
Ulmaceae

A large, water-loving elm; occasionally found near streams.

LEAVES: Upper surface very rough in both directions, 5–9 inches long, edges doubly serrate.

FLOWERS: Inconspicuous, in clusters, no petals, on short stalks; appear before the leaves; February–April.

FRUIT: Seeds surrounded by small wing, wing edges entire or slightly notched, ¼–¾ inch long, in clusters on short stalks; seeds mature late spring or early summer; minimum fruit-bearing age 15 years; will produce plentiful seed every 2–4 years and light seed crops in intervening years.

BARK: Gray to red brown, in flat ridges with deep furrows; solid brown when cut in cross section.

RANGE: Central Texas on the southwestern edge of range; throughout eastern United States from Texas north to Canada and east to Florida and Maine.

Although not common, slippery elm is a long-lived component of Central Texas riparian habitat and will grow best with protection from the west sun. In the right setting, it will grow with spreading branches forming a very wide crown. It is a host plant to question mark and mourning cloak butterflies.

Slippery elm gets its name from the inner bark, which is shiny and thick and forms a jelly when ground up and mixed with water. It has many medicinal properties and is sold in health-food stores to soothe cold symptoms. When steeped in hot water for about fifteen minutes, it makes a healthful, soothing tea.

Slippery elm can be distinguished from American elm in the following ways: slippery elm leaves are rough when stroked in both directions; the bark is solid brown when cut in cross section; and its seed wing edges are bare, entire, and borne on short stalks. In contrast, American elm leaves are sometimes rough when stroked toward the tip; the bark has light and dark lines when cut in cross section; and the seed wings are edged with tiny hairs, have a groove at the end, and hang on longer stalks.

Common Beebush, Whitebrush
Aloysia gratissima
Verbenaceae

Sweet, aromatic shrub with little white blossoms and many loose branches; often abundant on harsh, dry, rocky soil across the Edwards Plateau.

LEAVES: Small, simple, oval, opposite or usually in clusters, deciduous.

FLOWERS: Small, white, crowded on 3-inch spikes that arise from base of leaves; pleasant, fresh, vanilla scent; spring–fall after rain.

FRUIT: Small, with 2 small stones in each.

RANGE: New Mexico, South Texas, and Mexico.

This shrub can be used in landscaping as a thornless hedge or pruned into a small tree. It has many Spanish names that refer to its lovely scent. Beebush is poisonous to horses, mules, and donkeys, but it provides excellent dense cover for wildlife and good food for honeybees. The common name whitebrush refers to the fact that it will burst into bloom and be an outstanding white bush for several days following a good rain.

American Beautyberry
Callicarpa americana
Verbenaceae

A shade-loving shrub with many branches, usually 3–7 feet tall, which prefers moist woods and stream terraces.

LEAVES: Simple, large, broad, light green ovals with gradually pointed tips; grow in pairs or threes with coarsely toothed margins.

FLOWERS: White, pink, or bluish; appear in late spring and early summer.

FRUIT: Berrylike, showy, forming bright magenta (rarely white) clusters; fall.

RANGE: Bermuda, Cuba, and Florida north to Maryland and west to Bexar and Kendall counties in Central Texas.

American beautyberry is named for its unique combination of fall colors—light green leaves and vivid magenta fruit. Songbirds and small mammals eat American beautyberry fruit, and deer rarely touch its leaves. This attractive shrub is available in many nurseries that carry native species and is becoming a popular garden plant for shady spots. It can easily be reintroduced to riparian landscapes damaged by livestock or clearing.

Texas Lantana
Lantana urticoides (Lantana horrida)
Verbenaceae

Low, wide shrub, 2–6 feet tall, with many branches; common in pastures, thickets, hillsides, and fencerows.
LEAVES: Simple, opposite, broad ovals; pointed at the tip and flat at the base; with coarse teeth on the margins, upper surface rough to the touch.
FLOWERS: Small, in round, eye-catching, multicolored yellow, orange, and red clumps; blooms continually spring–fall.
FRUIT: Small, dark blue, fleshy; late summer–fall.
RANGE: In most of Texas except northwest, New Mexico, Arizona, and northern Mexico.

Texas lantana is widely used in landscaping as a colorful, low-growing shrub, resistant to drought and severe heat. Reportedly poisonous, the whole plant has a somewhat unpleasant, pungent aroma and taste that protect it from browsing deer. It does best in light, well-drained soil and can be propagated from seeds, cuttings, or long root sections.

Several other species or varieties of lantana, with different-colored flowers, have been imported from tropical America and are sold in local nurseries. These are not so resistant to freezing temperatures as is the native *L. urticoides.* Lantana contains an alkaloid called lantanine that suppresses fever and may relieve stomach distress. It is still used medicinally in Mexico. In the far western Mexican state of Sinaloa, the plant is a favorite remedy for snakebite. Leaves are crushed and made into a poultice applied to the wound and brewed into a tea for the snakebite victim. Texas lantana is a host plant to the painted lady butterfly. Hummingbirds and many different kinds of butterflies, including monarchs, drink nectar from its blossoms.

INVASIVE EXOTIC SPECIES

Chaste Tree
Vitex agnus-castus
Verbenaceae

Aromatic, deciduous sprawling shrub or small tree, 10–15 feet tall, usually with many trunks and a broad crown; becoming common near some streams and disturbed sites.

LEAVES: Alternate; with 5–7 narrow leaflets radiating from a central point, each leaflet tapered at both ends, longest leaflet up to 5 inches; upper surface dark green, lower surface covered with white hair.

FLOWERS: Small, lavender or white in dense cluster at end of a spike up to 7 inches long and extending beyond leaves; grow on new wood; May–October.

FRUIT: Small, round, dark brown; smells like pepper.

RANGE: Native to southern Europe and western Asia.

Chaste tree grows in alkaline soil and does well in part shade to full sun. It has been widely planted throughout Texas. An extract of the berries is commonly used today to treat menopausal symptoms and premenstrual syndrome.

Mistletoe, Injerto
Phoradendron tomentosum
Viscaceae

An evergreen parasite on trees throughout the Texas Hill Country; most visible on deciduous trees in the winter.

LEAVES: Opposite, simple, yellow-green, leathery, evergreen, edges smooth.

FLOWERS: Small, male and female on different plants; October–February.

FRUIT: Translucent white, sticky, 1 seed; ripen in winter.

RANGE: Southern United States and Mexico.

Mistletoe is a parasite that has chlorophyll in its leaves and stems and can also photosynthesize its own food. It seems to prefer trees with thin bark such as Spanish oak and netleaf hackberry. The part of mistletoe that penetrates a branch and removes nutrients often deforms or kills the branch. Mistletoe is poisonous to humans and can cause severe gastroenteritis and heart failure. However, some birds, such as cedar waxwings and eastern bluebirds, love the berries and are not harmed by them. Birds disperse mistletoe seed by wiping their beaks on the bark to remove the sticky seeds. It is host plant to the great purple hairstreak butterfly.

Cowitch Vine, Ivy Treebine
Cissus incisa
Vitaceae

A deciduous or nearly evergreen vine, climbing with tendrils that are opposite the leaves; grows on stream banks, rocky ravines, fences, shrubs, tree trunks, and old buildings.

LEAVES: Alternate, thick, fleshy; variable but usually with 3 lobes attached at a central point.

FLOWERS: Tiny, pale green-yellow, in flat clusters up to 2 inches across; June–July.

FRUIT: Small, round, green at first, dark blue–black when ripe, with 1–4 seeds, in clusters; ripen in summer.

RANGE: Throughout the Hill Country; north to Kansas and east to Florida; northern Mexico.

Cowitch vine's "leaves of three" mean that it can be confused with poison ivy, but *Cissus* leaves are fleshy and smelly when crushed. The berries are good wildlife food, and the plant's dense vine structure makes it excellent shelter for lizards. It grows well in deeper soils and could be used in wildscape gardening on a trellis, fence, or stone wall.

John Millsaps

Virginia Creeper
Parthenocissus quinquefolia
Vitaceae

An attractive vine with bright fall foliage, common in trees and along fencerows; sometimes confused with poison ivy.

LEAVES: Compound, up to 6 inches long; with 5 leaflets (rarely 7), all growing from the tip of the leaf stem, leaflets pointed and tapering to the base, margins with coarse teeth; turn brilliant red and orange in the fall.

FLOWERS: Small, green, in clusters; spring.

FRUIT: Small, round, blue, in loose clusters; late summer.

RANGE: Widespread from Texas, east to Florida, and north to Minnesota; Cuba, the Bahamas, and parts of Canada and Mexico.

"Leaves of five, let it thrive. Leaves of three, let them be." This is the rhyme used to tell Virginia creeper from poison ivy. Virginia creeper has five leaflets, and poison ivy has only three. Virginia creeper is a popular landscape vine, often growing in live oak trees, on a trellis, or across a stone wall. Its slender tendrils end in disks that fasten onto tree bark, rocks, or a wall. Virginia creeper has been cultivated since 1800. The bark was at one time used medicinally as an expectorant and as a treatment for dropsy. Its fruit is food for birds and small mammals.

Winter Grape, Spanish Grape
Vitis cinerea var. *helleri*
Vitaceae

Climbing grapevine with hanging grape clusters of small, sweet, thirst-quenching grapes; common in river bottoms; distinguished from mustang grape by smooth lower leaf surface.
LEAVES: Up to 4 inches long and 5 inches wide; with broad shallow teeth, pointed tip, often heart-shaped; smooth lower surface, veins on lower surface of mature leaves with white, cobweblike hairs that can be seen with a hand lens.

FLOWERS: Tiny, yellow-green, in clusters up to 8 inches long; April–May.
FRUIT: Small, green at first, then reddish purple; usually more than 25 in a bunch, edible; August–October.
RANGE: Variety seems to be limited to Central Texas and the Trans-Pecos.

Another grape species, *V. monticola,* also grows in the Hill Country and is easily confused with *V. cinerea.* They are difficult to distinguish, but *V. cinerea* has larger grape clusters and leaves, and each grape cluster has more grapes.

Mustang Grape
Vitis mustangensis
Vitaceae

Very common grapevine, climbing over bushes and high into tall trees; easily identified by its broad leaves with downy white hair on the underside.

LEAVES: Of two types: most common type generally heart-shaped with coarse teeth on the margins; other type with deep lobes, found on rapidly growing shoots in bright sun; upper surface dull dark green, lower surface covered with white woolly hairs.

FLOWERS: In clusters 2–3 inches long; spring.

FRUIT: Sour, dark purple grapes, ½–¾ inch in diameter depending on rainfall; largest wild grapes in Hill Country; ripen June–September.

RANGE: From southwestern Texas north to Oklahoma and east to Louisiana and Arkansas.

Mustang grapes are sour but can be used to make jelly and wine. This is a vigorous drought-, heat-, and disease-resistant vine. Near streams, old vines may be more than 40 feet long with a trunk base as large as that of a tree. There are two other species of wild grapes in the Texas Hill Country. Their leaves have a shape similar to those of the mustang grape but are thinner and lack white fuzz on the lower surface. Their grapes are also much smaller and sweet. All grapes are good food for birds, deer, and small mammals.

Guayacan, Soapbush
Guajacum angustifolium
Zygophyllaceae

An unusual, xeric, evergreen shrub with branches so short that the tiny leaves seem to be growing out of the stem; found mostly to the south and west of the Hill Country, but some on the Edwards Plateau as far north as Austin.

LEAVES: Pinnately compound, 4–8 pairs of tiny leaflets that grow in tight clusters.

FLOWERS: Abundant, about 1 inch wide, 5 violet-purple petals, fragrant; March–April.

FRUIT: Yellow capsule containing 1–3 shiny red seeds.

RANGE: From southern edge of Edwards Plateau through South Texas brush country and the Trans-Pecos into northern Mexico.

Guayacan has extremely hard wood, which is used for tool handles, fence posts, and barbecue wood. Where this plant grows in northern Mexico, markets sell soapbush root bark. It is especially good for washing wool blankets and winter garments because its soap does not shrink the wool fiber. An extract made from guayacan roots has also been used to treat arthritis and venereal disease.

For native plant gardening, guayacan is a good choice as a hedge or stand-alone bush in sunny locations with poor soil. Although slow growing in its natural dry habitat, guayacan will grow more rapidly with a little watering and does not need fertilizer. Bees drink nectar from the flowers; swallowtail, gray hairstreak, and lyside sulphur butterfly caterpillars live on its leaves; deer browse its leaves and branches; small mammals hide in its dense cover; and birds nest in its branches.

Anne Adams

CLASS: LILIOPSIDA

Texas Sotol
Dasylirion texanum
Agavaceae
A bright green, dense clump made of long, narrow leaves with spiny edges; common in colonies on exposed rocky slopes.

LEAVES: Flat, slender, 3 feet long; with claws on both edges, all curved toward the leaf tip; each with a broad base hidden within the clump.

FLOWERS: Tiny in a large, dense, yellow to tan cluster on the upper few feet of a stalk 8 feet tall; late summer–early fall.

FRUIT: Capsules, each with 3 wings and 1 seed.

RANGE: Only in Central Texas from New Braunfels west to Fort Davis.

Sotol, a distinctive xeriscape plant that is attractive in native landscaping, was a food source for the Lipan Indians and early Texas settlers. They called the plant soto root, soto grass, or wild artichoke and made ovens in the ground to roast it. The cooks would dig a hole, fill it with rocks, and then burn brush and leaves atop the rocks until they were hot. Then the soto roots would be sprinkled among the rocks, covered, and left to bake for several days.

Sotol leaves grow from a bulb just beneath the surface of the ground. The Lipans also made a kind of flour out of sotol bulbs that they first cooked and then sun-dried. Then they ground the bulbs into white flour, using wooden pestles to work the mixture held in the large holes of a rock or a log. The cook mixed this flour with water to form a paste that was shaped into little cakes and baked. Today, sotol leaves and heart are used as emergency food by deer and javelinas, and the tender young stalks are a favorite deer browse.

Devil's Shoestring, Ribbon Grass
Nolina lindheimeriana
Agavaceae

Makes a large, grasslike clump that grows in partial shade or sun on limestone cliffs and slopes, but unlike grass, is evergreen.

LEAVES: Flat, 30 inches long and ¼ inch wide; margins finely saw-toothed; grow from ground level or low part of stem.

FLOWERS: White to cream, tiny; numerous on slender, loose branches off a stem 2–3 feet tall; April–May.

FRUIT: Small, dark blue capsules, less than ¼ inch wide; ripen in summer.

RANGE: Edwards Plateau.

N. lindheimeriana is very similar to *N. texana*. The differences are that *N. lindheimeriana* makes a thinner clump with fewer leaves; its flower stalk is tall, extending high above the plant; and its leaves have fine, saw-toothed edges. The species name recognizes Ferdinand Lindheimer, who collected plants in Texas and sent them to experts in the United States and Europe for identification. He settled in New Braunfels, where there is a small, charming museum in his honor.

Beargrass, Sacahuista
Nolina texana
Agavaceae
Looks like a large, thick clump of
very coarse grass, but unlike grass, is
evergreen; easy to spot on ledges and
rocky slopes.
LEAVES: Rounded with one flat side,
   numerous, 3–4 feet long and
   ¼ inch wide, evergreen; grow
   from a hidden, central woody
   base and drape to the ground.
FLOWERS: Small, off-white, on short
   stalks that barely emerge from the
   top of the leaf clump; March–late
   July.
FRUIT: Tiny, spherical seeds in small,
   thin-walled, 3-lobed capsules;
   ripen in summer.

RANGE: From Central Texas south to
   the Rio Grande Plains and west to
   the Trans-Pecos.

Beargrass grows back very quickly
after fire, and the new leaves are
eaten by deer. Flowers are poisonous,
causing liver-kidney toxicity in cattle.
Beargrass is eaten by cattle only when
other food is not present.

Buckley's Yucca
Yucca constricta
Agavaceae

With long, curly threads on the leaf margins and a short, stout spine on the leaf tip, this yucca grows in a tight ball, scattered in openings among brush.

LEAVES: Very slender, up to 2 feet long and ⅝ inch wide; stiff, with sharp points and long, curly threads on margins; grow from a center usually on or near the ground.

FLOWERS: Showy, greenish white, bell-shaped in a branched cluster at top of tall stalk; April–June.

FRUIT: Brown or black capsule, opening from the tip.

RANGE: Edwards Plateau, south across Rio Grande Plains, and west into the Trans-Pecos.

All yucca species are pollinated by a yucca moth that flies at dusk. The female yucca moth first collects yucca pollen from the male part of a flower and packs it into a ball under her neck. Then she visits another flower, where she lays twenty to thirty eggs into each immature yucca seed. Finally, she climbs to the female part of the flower, where she spreads the pollen she has collected. Thus, she assures development of seeds that are food for her larval offspring. Each larva will destroy the seed where it grows and those it eats, but many undamaged ones remain with the potential of reproducing the yucca plant. Buckley's yucca is a host plant for yucca giant skipper butterfly.

Another yucca species, *Y. arkansana,* grows in the Texas Hill Country, and it could be confused with *Y. constricta;* however, this plant does not have the tight ball shape, its flower cluster is usually unbranched or has only one or two short branches at its base, and its leaves are wider.

Twist Leaf Yucca
Yucca rupicola
Agavaceae
Most common yucca in the Texas Hill
Country; easily identified by long,
coarse, twisting leaves growing from
a central point near the ground;
found in grassland, open woods,
brush country, and canyon ledges.
LEAVES: Slender, 1–2 feet long, stiff,
    dark green; terminal spine, often
    twisted; edges tan or yellow with
    tiny sharp teeth.

FLOWERS: Large, creamy white,
    succulent, bell-shaped, fragrant;
    on stalk 2 to more than 5 feet tall;
    April–June.
FRUIT: Tiny, dull black seeds, in
    brown capsules 2–3 inches long;
    on upper portion of tall flower
    stalk.
RANGE: Endemic to southeastern Ed-
    wards Plateau; especially common
    in Gillespie, Kerr, Kendall, Travis,
    Hays, and Comal counties.

Twist leaf yucca's species name means
"lover of rocks." *Yucca* is an American
genus of thirty-five species found
in arid regions. It was an important
resource for Native Americans of the
Southwest. Native peoples ate emerging yucca flower buds and flowers
raw or boiled and roasted its flower
stalks. They made rope, mats, sandals, baskets, and cloth from yucca
leaf fiber. Twist leaf yucca is a host
plant for the yucca giant skipper
butterfly. Its seeds are eaten by birds
and rodents. White-tailed deer love
its flower stalks, buds, and flowers.

Spanish Dagger
Yucca treculeana
Agavaceae

A treelike yucca, usually on a single, sometimes leafy trunk; may be a few branches at the top of mature plants; found on southern edge of the Edwards Plateau.

LEAVES: Swordlike, thick, rigid, 2 ½–4 feet long and 1–3 ½ inches wide, silver-green or blue-green; stout spine at tip, smooth upper surface; in clumps at end of stubby branches.

FLOWERS: Cream-colored, fragrant, waxy; in huge eye-catching clusters at end of stalk; usually in alternate years; usually March–April.

FRUIT: Reddish brown capsule, 2–4 inches long; many flat, black, triangular seeds; seeds mature in fall.

RANGE: Southwestern plant from southern part of Edwards Plateau, throughout the Rio Grande Plains, and south into northern Mexico.

Spanish dagger grows as an exotic ornamental shrub on the Ligurian coast of Italy, where it has escaped cultivation. Its size, up to 20 feet tall, and fierce, elegant character make Spanish dagger a memorable plant. If you plant one, do not put it anywhere near a sidewalk, driveway, or location where children play. Native Americans used the trunks as stockades; made soap from its roots for washing clothes and hair; and used its fiber for cloth, baskets, mats, paper, rope, and sandals. Young flower stalks, buds, and flowers can be eaten raw, boiled, or pickled like cabbage. Flowers are excellent when sautéed with onions. Birds such as cactus wrens, Inca doves, and mockingbirds nest in the protection of Spanish dagger leaves. Deer eat the blossoms, and it is a host plant for its pollinator, the yucca moth.

Photo by Anne Adams

Bush Palmetto, Dwarf Palmetto
Sabal minor
Arecaceae

Rarely grows a trunk, so always looks like a very young palm; found in low, moist places; only palm native to the Texas Hill Country.

LEAVES: Fan-shaped, up to 4 feet wide, arising from an underground root stock; deep fingers on leaf blades with shallow indentations on the ends, blades longer than stalks.

FLOWERS: Numerous, small, white in showy clusters; summer.

FRUIT: Hard, black, spherical seed, ½ inch in diameter.

RANGE: From Texas Hill Country north into Oklahoma and Arkansas and east to North Carolina; abundant in river bottoms and swamps of southern Louisiana.

Bush palmetto is browsed by cattle. The fruit are edible and eaten by birds and mammals. It is not a xeric plant and grows only in moist places with rich alluvial soil.

Ball Moss
Tillandsia recurvata
Bromeliaceae
An epiphyte that can live with very little water; most common on live oaks but also grows on other trees as well as rocks and utility wires.

LEAVES: Arise from a center point, gray or gray-green when moist; curve outward, long and slender, covered with scales.

FLOWERS: Several per plant, bluish, tiny, on slender stalks; bloom throughout year.

RANGE: Central and South Texas, Arizona, Louisiana, and Florida; south to Argentina.

Ball moss is in the pineapple or bromeliad family. Most species in this family live in the tropics of the New World. As an epiphyte, ball moss does *not* harm the plant it grows on. It is not necessary to remove ball moss to protect or improve the health of live oak trees. The plants are removed only for aesthetic reasons by landowners who do not like the look of epiphytes on their trees.

Ball moss contains chlorophyll and uses photosynthesis to make its food from the sun and the small amount of moisture it collects. Wet a sample, and you will see a sudden transformation from gray to pale green. Ball moss is temperature sensitive and has expanded its range northward in the last eighty years. It may be an early indicator species of changing climatic conditions in this region. Ball moss is a refuge for insects, especially during dry seasons.

INVASIVE EXOTIC SPECIES

Giant Reed
Arundo donax
Poaceae
Neither a reed nor a tree but a grass, included here because it is as large as a tree and is an invasive alien impacting ponds and roadsides.

LEAVES: Long and narrow, 1 ½–3 inches wide on main leaf stems.

FLOWERS: Flower head 12–24 inches long, maturing from base to tip; October–November.

RANGE: Native to Mediterranean region; naturalized and spread throughout the southern United States and as far north as Illinois.

Giant reed commonly stands 7–20 feet tall. It grows in dense, clay soil where it spreads, forming huge, thick clumps that physically exclude native species. In the Texas Hill Country, it is often seen along highways where it has been cultivated. Giant reed reproduces by underground stems and stem fragments that are easily spread by water. It also resprouts quickly after burning and has the potential to expand quickly, covering hundreds of acres. Giant reed is listed as an invasive weed by USDI, Geological Survey 1996 and Southeast Exotic Pest Plant Council 1999. Giant reed is mentioned in the Bible and has been used to make musical instruments for over five thousand years. It is still the source of "wood" for the reeds of wind instruments.

Greenbrier
Smilax bona-nox
Smilacaceae

Tough, spiny vine with smooth, green stems that have sharp prickles, forming dense tangles in shrubby wooded areas and considered a common "garden thug."

LEAVES: Simple, late deciduous; surfaces green and smooth and sometimes mottled; shape variable from triangular to heartlike; thick, firm texture.

FLOWERS: Small, inconspicuous, in clusters emerging from leaf base; male and female on different plants; March–June.

FRUIT: Spherical, individual or in small clumps, fleshy; green at first, then turns dark blue-black; matures September–November.

RANGE: From Texas across eastern United States and south into Mexico.

Greenbrier climbs with tendrils and has an extensive root system that makes it difficult to eliminate from a garden. Try eating the tender new growth in the spring while the weather is still cool. It is a tasty wild salad. Greenbrier is a favorite deer browse. Dense thickets of greenbrier mixed with other understory species may form in the absence of deer and goats. These thickets serve as excellent cover for cottontails and other small mammals.

Plant Chart

We preserve native plants for many different reasons. Many choose to use native plants in landscaping. Some of us wish to maintain native trees, shrubs, and vines in order to provide natural forage and cover for deer. Others have a special interest in birds or butterflies and want to exclude deer. Whatever the reason, we are wise to clarify priorities so we can make decisions that will support our personal choices. The information in the plant chart is intended to help land managers know and choose the right plant for the right reason.

204

Name	Color or Aroma	Season	Potential Height	Site Preference	Wildlife Use
Ashe Juniper *Juniperus ashei*	blue berries	winter	20–30 ft	dry hillsides, rocky ground	birds, small mammals
Mexican Pinyon *Pinus edulis*	small, round cones	February	12–36 ft	dry, alkaline soil part shade	turkeys, scrub jays, other birds
Bald Cypress *Taxodium distichum*	orange-brown fall foliage	spring	over 100 ft	in or near streams	ducks, small mammals
Bigtooth Maple *Acer grandidentatum var. sinuosom*	brilliant fall foliage	spring	45 ft	shady canyons, steep stream banks	birds, deer
Box Elder *Acer negundo*		spring	70 ft	understory, near streams	birds, squirrels
American Smoke Tree *Cotinus obovatus*	brilliant fall foliage	spring	25 ft	dry hills, high bluffs	deer
Aromatic Sumac *Rhus aromatica*	aromatic foliage	spring	8 ft	rocky, dry soil	bees
Flameleaf Sumac *Rhus lanceolata*	bright red fall foliage	summer	20 ft	fencerows, old fields, rocky hillsides	songbirds, quail, butterflies, deer
Desert Sumac *Rhus microphylla*	small white blossoms	spring	3–10 ft	dry brushland	birds, small mammals, lizards

Plant	Description	Season	Size	Habitat	Wildlife
Evergreen Sumac *Rhus virens*	white blossoms, red berries	summer	12 ft	rocky slopes, gullies	songbirds, quail, butterflies, deer
Poison Ivy *Toxicodendron radicans*	small, white fruit	fall	climbing disturbed ground	woodland edges, butterflies	deer, birds,
Possumhaw *Ilex decidua*	red-orange berries	fall, winter	20 ft	bottomland, fencerows, thickets	birds, butterflies, small mammals, deer
Yaupon Holly *Ilex vomitoria*	red berries	fall, *winter*	20 ft	along stream, in canyons	birds
Bearded Swallowwort *Cynanchum barbigerum*	tiny cream-colored blossoms	spring, summer	climbing to 6 ft	high fencerows, brush	deer, variegated fritillary butterflies
Pearl Milkweed *Matelea reticulata*	delicate green blossoms	summer, fall	climbing to 12 ft	open woodland, fencerows, thickets	monarch butterflies
Wavy Leaf Milkweed Vine *Sarcostemma crispum*	dark rust red blossoms	spring, summer, fall	climbing to 6 ft	fencerows, thickets	queen butterflies
Poverty Bush *Baccharis neglecta*	silky white blossoms	fall	9 ft	dry pastures, fallow fields	insects
Damianita *Chrysactinia mexicana*	bright yellow blossoms	spring, summer, early fall	low, 16 in	disturbed ground	butterflies

Name	Color or Aroma	Season	Potential Height	Site Preference	Wildlife Use
Texas Barberry *Berberis swaseyi*	fragrant yellow blossoms	spring	4 ft	variable, best in bottomland	birds, butterflies
Agarita *Berberis trifoliata*	yellow blossoms, red berries	late winter, early spring	4–6 ft	thickets, rocky dry ground	birds, butterflies, small mammals
Trumpet Creeper *Campsis radicans*	large orange blossoms	late spring, early fall	climbing	bottomland	hummingbirds, deer
Desert Willow *Chilopsis linearis*	large, pink blossom	late spring–early fall	30 ft	near streams, in dry creek beds	hummingbirds, bees
Anaqua *Ehretia anacua*	fragrant white blossoms	spring	30 ft	bottomland	bees, birds
Tasajillo *Opuntia leptocaulis*	yellow blossoms, red fruit	late spring, early summer	5 ft	bottomland deer	birds, small mammals, deer
White Honeysuckle *Lonicera albiflora*	white blossoms, red berries	spring	climbing	fencerows, rocky hillsides	birds, butterflies, small mammals, deer
Coral Honeysuckle *Lonicera sempervirens*	red blossoms	spring–fall	twining, does not spread	fencerows, part sun	hummingbirds
Common Elderberry *Sambucus canadensis*	white blossoms	late spring–summer	10 ft	moist soil, along streams	birds

Name	Blossom / Fruit	Bloom	Size	Habitat	Wildlife
Rusty Blackhaw *Viburnum rufidulum*	white blossoms, fall color	spring	12 ft	woodlands, fencerows, ponds	birds, bees, deer
Texas Bindweed *Convolvulus equitans*	white blossoms	spring, summer, fall	twining to 6 ft	thickets	birds, lizards, small mammals
Wild Morning Glory *Ipomoea cordatotriloba*	lavender blossoms	spring, summer, fall	low twining	sun, disturbed ground	birds, lizards, small mammals
Lindheimer's Morning Glory *Ipomoea lindheimeri*	large lavender blossoms	spring, summer, fall	twining to 6 ft	sun or shade, thickets, dry fencerows	birds, lizards, small mammals
Alamo Vine *Merremia dissecta*	large white blossoms	spring, summer, fall	twining into large mass	disturbed soil, bottomland	birds, lizards, small mammals
Rough Leaf Dogwood *Cornus drummondii*	creamy white blossoms and fruit	spring	25 ft	moist stream banks, bottomlands	songbirds, turkeys, quail, small mammals
Buffalo Gourd *Cucurbita foetidissima*	striped gourds, yellow blossoms	spring, summer, fall	sprawling, 20 ft	disturbed ground, roadsides	bees
Texas Persimmon *Diospyros texana*	blue-black fruit	spring	30 ft	thickets, hillsides, dry open woods	turkeys, foxes, raccoon, ringtails, butterflies
Texas Madrone *Arbutus xalapensis*	white blossoms, red fruit	early spring	20 ft	limestone hillsides, with Ashe juniper	birds, bees, small mammals, deer

Name	Color or Aroma	Season	Potential Height	Site Preference	Wildlife Use
Southwest Bernardia *Bernardia myricifolia*	gray-brown seedpods	late spring, early summer	3–8 ft	full sun, drought tolerant, dry rocky soil	birds, Lacey's scrub-hairstreak butterfly
Bush Croton *Croton fruticulosis*	very small flower	summer–fall	3 ft	in brush on hills and canyons	goatweed and gray hairstreak butterflies
Huisache *Acacia minuata*	fragrant yellow-gold blossoms	spring	30 ft	sunny pastures, fencerows	butterflies, bees
Catclaw *Acacia roemeriana*	fragrant cream-colored blossoms	spring	9 ft	rocky ground, canyons, hills, prairies	butterflies, bees
False Indigo *Amorpha fruticosa*	dark spikes	spring	8 ft	partial shade, good drainage, some moisture	gray hairstreak butterflies
Texas Redbud *Cercis canadensis* var. *texensis*	pink blossoms	spring	20 ft	sun or part shade, dry, rocky soil, bottomland	butterflies, bees, deer
Black Dalea *Dalea frutescens*	bright purple blossoms	summer, fall	3 ft	full sun, dry, rocky fields, roadsides	butterflies, bees
Texas Kidneywood *Eysenhardtia texana*	fragrant white blossoms	late spring, summer, fall	12 ft	sun, streams, woodlands, roadsides	butterflies, bees, deer
Golden Ball Lead Tree *Leucaena retusa*	yellow blossoms	spring	15 ft	dry, rocky hillsides	butterflies, bees

Name	Description	Bloom	Height	Habitat	Wildlife
Pink Mimosa *Mimosa borealis*	bright pink blossoms	spring	6 ft	full sun, dry, rough ground, hillsides	butterflies, bees, birds
Retama *Parkinsonia aculeata*	yellow-orange blossoms	spring, summer, fall	35 ft	fencerows, disturbed places	butterflies, bees, birds
Honey Mesquite *Prosopis glandulosa* var. *glandulosa*	yellow-green spikes	spring, summer	20–30 ft	old pastures, fallow fields	butterflies, bees, dove
Eve's Necklace *Sophora affinis*	fragrant pink blossoms	spring	18 ft	open woods, fencerows, thickets	butterflies, bees, small mammals, deer
Texas Mountain Laurel *Sophora secundiflora*	large, fragrant blue-purple blossoms	late winter, spring	12 ft	limestone hills	butterflies, bees
Spanish Oak *Quercus buckleyi*	dark orange-red fall foliage	spring	15–30 ft	dry uplands	birds, small mammals, deer
Lacey Oak *Quercus laceyi*	blue-green foliage	spring	20–30 ft	limestone hills, canyons	birds, small mammals, deer
Bur Oak *Quercus macrocarpa*	huge leaves and acorns	fall	40–100 ft	part shade to full sun	birds, deer, other mammals; Edwards' hairstreak and Horace's duskywing butterflies
Blackjack Oak *Quercus marilandica*	dark red-brown fall foliage	fall	30 ft	dry gravel, sandy soil	deer, turkeys

Name	Color or Aroma	Season	Potential Height	Site Preference	Wildlife Use
Chinkapin Oak *Quercus muhlenbergii*	some yellow foliage		40–60 ft	well-drained slopes near streams	deer, turkeys, squirrels, raccoon
Shin Oak *Quercus sinuata*	brown	fall	30 ft	dry, shallow or deeper soil	deer, small mammals
Post Oak *Quercus stellata*	brown	fall	40–50 ft	dry uplands, acid soil	birds, small mammals, deer
Live Oak *Quercus virginiana var. fusiformis*	green	all year	40–50 ft high, 50–80 ft wide	bottomlands, caliche	birds, butterflies, deer
Lindheimer's Silktassel *Garrya ovata subsp. lindheimeri*	dusty pink blossoms, blue fruit	spring	20 ft	rocky slopes, stream banks	birds
Witch Hazel *Hamamelis virginiana*	small yellow blossoms	fall, early winter	20 ft	understory, near streams	birds, small mammals, deer
Texas Buckeye *Aesculus glabra var. arguta*	pale yellow blossoms	spring	10–30 ft	full sun, near streams	hummingbirds, song bird
Pale Buckeye *Aesculus pavia var. flavescens*	yellow blossoms	spring	10 ft	shade, moist soil, thickets, canyons	hummingbirds, song birds

Plant	Features	Bloom	Height	Habitat	Wildlife
Canyon Mock Orange *Philadelphus ernestii*	white blossoms	spring	4 ft	shade, moist soil	bees
Pecan *Carya illinoinensis*			over 100 ft	rich bottomland, near streams	cecropia moths, turkeys, small mammals
Little Walnut *Juglans microcarpa*			30 ft	along streams, dry ravines	cecropia moths, squirrels, javelinas
Spicebush *Lindera benzoin*	yellow fall foliage, red berries	early spring	10–15 ft	moist bottomland, dappled shade	birds
Turk's Cap *Malvaviscus drummondii*	red blossoms	summer, fall November	5 ft	shade, moist soil	birds (especially hummingbirds), butterflies
Rose Pavonia *Pavonia lasiopetala*	pink blossoms	April–November	2–3 feet	part shade to full sun; well-drained soil; caliche, clay, or loam	deer
Carolina Snailseed *Cocculus carolinus*	red berries	summer	climbing, twining	fencerows, thickets	migrant birds, deer
Bois d'Arc *Maclura pomifera*	large green fruit	spring, early summer	40 ft	fencerows, near streams	squirrels
Texas Mulberry *Morus microphylla*	white/red/black fruit	spring	15 ft	partial shade, rocky slopes, near streams	birds, butterflies, small mammals

Name	Color or Aroma	Season	Potential Height	Site Preference	Wildlife Use
Red Mulberry *Morus rubra*	red fruit	spring	40 ft	bottomland, moist woods	birds, small mammals
Elbow Bush *Forestiera pubescens*	small pale yellow blossoms	late winter, early spring	15 ft	fencerows, open woods, near streams	bees, birds, small mammals
Texas Ash *Fraxinus texensis*		early spring	30 ft	light shade, rocky slopes, canyons, bluffs	birds, small mammals
Bracted Passion Flower *Passiflora affinis*	yellow-green		climbing	moist woods, steep canyons	zebra longwing and gulf fritillary butterflies
Spreadlobe Passion Flower *Passiflora tenuiloba*	small, intricate pale blossoms	spring, summer, fall	low climber	fencerows, thickets	zebra longwing and gulf fritillary butterflies
American Sycamore *Platanus occidentalis*		spring	100 ft	bottomland, canyons, springs	birds, deer
Old Man's Beard *Clematis drummondii*	seeds with silky white plumes	summer, fall	climbing	fencerows, dry soil	deer
Redroot *Ceanothus herbaceus*	white blossoms	spring	3 ft	rocky banks, woodlands, open fields	quail, deer

Name	Characteristics	Season	Height	Soil/Light	Wildlife
Hog Plum *Colubrina texensis*	unusual star-shaped blossoms	spring	3–6 ft	shallow, rocky soil	deer, birds, small mammals, javelinas
Green Condalia *Condalia viridis*	bright green leaves	seeds ripen in summer	3–9 ft	full sun	birds
Carolina Buckthorn *Frangula caroliniana*	yellow, red, black fruit	late spring, early summer	25 ft	sun or shade, fencerows, streams	birds, small mammals, deer
Coyotillo *Karwinskia humboltiana*	evergreen	seeds in summer–fall	2–20 ft	part shade to full sun	birds, coyotes
Mountain Mahogany *Cercocarpus montanus*	silver leaves and plumed fruit	late summer–fall	to 12 ft	full sun	deer, mountain mahogany hairstreak
Hawthorn *Crataegus sp.*	white blossoms	spring	16 ft	bottomland near moisture	bees, deer
Blanco Crabapple *Maleus ioënsis var. texensis*	large pink blossoms	spring	15 ft	bottomland, canyon heads, springs	birds, bees, deer
Texas Almond *Prunus minutiflora*	small cream-colored blossoms	late winter–early spring	3 ft	dry slopes	birds, small mammals
Creek Plum *Prunus rivularis*	white blossoms	late winter, early spring	6 ft	lowland fencerows, creek bottoms	birds, bees, deer, butterflies, small mammals

Name	Color or Aroma	Season	Potential Height	Site Preference	Wildlife Use
Escarpment Black Cherry *Prunus serotina* var. *eximia*	white blossoms	spring	40 ft	hillsides, canyons	birds, bees, deer, butterflies, small mammals
Dewberry *Rubus riograndis*	white blossoms, purple berries	spring	trailing	bottomland	birds, box turtles, small mammals, deer
Common Buttonbush *Cephalanthus occidetalis*	white blossoms	summer, early fall	7 ft	wet soil, near streams, springs	ducks, bees, butterflies
Wafer Ash *Ptelea trifoliata*	aromatic blossoms and foliage	spring	6 ft	fencerows, woodland edges	birds, swallowtail butterflies
Tickle Tongue *Zanthoxylum hirsutum*	aromatic foliage, red-brown fruit	early spring	8 ft	rocky, dry soil	bees, birds, small mammals
Cottonwood *Populus deltoides*			100 ft	near streams, springs	birds, small mammals, deer
Black Willow *Salix nigra*			40 ft	sun or part shade, wet bottomland	hummingbirds, herons, kingfishers, Texas viceroy butterfly
Western Soapberry *Sapindus saponaria* var. *drummondii*	cream-colored blossoms	spring, summer	30 ft	sunny fencerows, woodland edges	butterflies

Name	Feature	Season	Height	Habitat	Wildlife
Mexican Buckeye *Ungnadia speciosa*	bright pink blossoms	spring	15 ft	shady canyons, creek banks	butterflies, bees
Gum Bumelia *Sideroxylon lanuginosum*	small purple-black fruit	fall	15–40 ft	dry rocky soil, fencerows, open woods	birds, small mammals, deer
Cenizo *Leucophyllum frutescens*	gray foliage, lavender-pink blossoms	late spring, summer, fall	8 ft	rocky hillsides, bluffs	butterflies, bees
Snapdragon Vine *Maurandya antirrhiniflora*	purple–dark blue blossoms	spring, summer, fall	twining, 3–10 ft	rocky soil, brushland	insects, lizards
Sycamore Leaf Snowbell *Styrax platanifolius*	big white blossoms	spring	12 ft	steep bluffs, near streams	deer
Linden *Tilia americana* var. *caroliniana*	fragrant blossoms	late spring–early summer	50 ft	fertile soil, valleys, near streams	bees, small mammals
Netleaf Hackberry *Celtis laevigata* var. *reticulata*		spring	20–50 ft	bottomland, dry ground, fencerows	birds, butterflies, small mammals, deer
Cedar Elm *Ulmus crassifolia*	yellow fall color	late summer, fall	50 ft	open woods	turkey, small mammals, deer

Name	Color or Aroma	Season	Potential Height	Site Preference	Wildlife Use
Slippery Elm *Ulmus rubra*			65 ft	near streams	birds, small mammals, deer
Common Beebush *Aloysia gratissima*	white blossoms	spring, summer, fall	9 ft	harsh, dry, rocky uplands	butterflies, bees
American Beautyberry *Callicarpa americana*	magenta berries	late spring, early summer	7 ft	moist woods, stream banks	birds, small mammals, deer
Texas Lantana *Lantana urticoides*	yellow, orange, red blossoms	spring, summer, fall	6 ft	dry fencerows, pastures, hillsides	birds, butterflies, hummingbirds
Mistletoe *Phoradendron tomentosum*	white fruit	winter	climbing	parasite on thin bark	birds
Cowitch Vine *Cissus incisa*	dark blue–black fruit	summer	climbing	stream banks, rocky ravines	birds, small mammals
Virginia Creeper *Parthenocissus quinquefolia*	brilliant fall foliage	spring	climbing	sun or part shade, in trees, fencerows	butterflies, birds, small mammals, deer
Winter Grape *Vitis cinerea var. helleri*	red-purple grapes	spring	climbing	fencerows, thickets	birds, small mammals

Plant	Flowers	Bloom	Size	Habitat	Wildlife
Mustang Grape *Vitis mustangensis*	large dark purple grapes	spring	climbing, spreading	sun or shade, fencerows, bottomland in trees	birds, raccoon, deer, ringtails, foxes
Guayacan *Guaiacum angustifolium*	fragrant violet blossoms	spring	8–10 ft	full sun, well-drained soil	bees, swallowtail butterflies, deer, small mammals, birds
Texas Sotol *Dasylirion texanum*	large white blossoms	late summer –early fall	leaves 2 ft, flower stalk 8 ft	dry, rocky hillsides	deer
Devil's Shoestring *Nolina lindheimeriana*	tiny white flowers	spring	leaves 2½ ft, flower stalk 3 ft	part sun or shade, roadsides, cliffs, slopes	deer
Beargrass *Nolina texana*	tiny white flowers	spring– summer	leaves 3 ft	ledges, rocky slopes	deer
Buckley's Yucca *Yucca constricta*	showy greenish white blossoms	spring, early summer	10 ft	in dry brush	moths, birds, deer
Twist Leaf Yucca *Yucca rupicola*	white blossoms	spring, early summer	leaves 2 ft, flower stalk 5 ft	sun or shade, dry soil	moths, birds, deer
Spanish Dagger *Yucca treculeana*	large cream-colored blossoms	spring	20 ft	open areas in brush	moths, birds, deer
Bush Palmetto *Sabal minor*	showy, white clusters	summer	4 ft	wet, lowland shade	birds, small mammals

Name	Color or Aroma	Season	Potential Height	Site Preference	Wildlife Use
Ball Moss *Tillandsia recurvata*	tiny bluish blossoms	all seasons	epiphyte	on tree branches, telephone wires	insects, birds
Greenbrier *Smilax bona-nox*		spring, early summer	climbing, twining	sun or shade, bottomland thickets	birds, small mammals, deer

RESOURCES

Native Plant Society of Texas

If you are interested in preserving native species on your land, the Native Plant Society of Texas has well-informed amateurs and professionals among its members, who can provide a wealth of information and assistance.

Native Plant Society of Texas
Dana Tucker
P.O. Box 891
Georgetown, TX 78627
Phone: (512) 868-8799
E-mail: dtucker@io.com
Web site: www.npsot.org

Native Plant Society of Texas, Austin Chapter
David Heberling
Austin, TX
Phone: (512) 922-3744
Meets third Tuesday, 7 P.M., Wild Basin Wilderness, 805 N. Capital of Texas Hwy.

Native Plant Society of Texas, Bandera Chapter
Sandra Magee
Medina, TX
Phone: (830) 589-7549
Meets first Thursday, 7 P.M., Bandera Public Library

Native Plant Society of Texas, Boerne Chapter
Rebecca Rogers
Boerne, TX 78006
Phone: (830) 249-9343
Meets first Tuesday, 7 P.M., Cibolo Nature Center

Native Plant Society of Texas, Fredericksburg Chapter
Lonnie Childs
Fredericksburg, TX 78624
Phone: (830) 685-3811
Meets last Tuesday, 7 P.M., Gillespie County Historical Society

Native Plant Society of Texas, Georgetown Chapter
Sue Wiseman
Phone: (512) 259-4106
Meets second Thursday, 7 P.M., Williamson County Maintenance Facility

Native Plant Society of Texas, Kerrville Chapter
John Quinby
Kerrville, TX
Phone: (830) 367-4612
Meets first Tuesday, 2 P.M., Riverside Nature Center

Native Plant Society of Texas, New Braunfels Chapter
Larry Maroney
New Braunfels, TX
Phone: (830) 626-7848
Meets third Tuesday, 7 P.M., GVTC Bldg., 36101 FM 3159, Smithson
Valley, TX

Native Plant Society of Texas, San Antonio Chapter
Melissa Miller
San Antonio, TX 78209
Phone: (210) 302-3698
Meets fourth Tuesday, 7 P.M., Lions Club Field House
Web site: www.npsot.org/SanAntonio

Native Plant Experts

Experts on native plants, land management, and landscaping have different areas of expertise. The services of federal and state agencies are free. Others usually charge a modest hourly fee. Keep looking until you find the individual who can best help with your needs.

City of San Antonio
Janis Merritt, Native Plant Specialist
Natural Areas Division
21395 Milsa Rd., San Antonio, TX 78256
Phone: (210) 698-1057

Green Cloud Nursery
Chuck Janzow, Native Plant Specialist
Boerne, TX 78006
Phone: (830) 249-3844

Patty Leslie-Pasztor, Range Consultant and Native Plant Specialist
126 Calumet Place
San Antonio, TX 78209-3317
Phone: (210) 824-1235

San Antonio Botanical Gardens
Paul Cox and Scott Litchke, Native Plant Specialists
555 Funston Place
San Antonio, TX 78209
Phone: Paul (210) 207-3264; Scott (210) 207-3275

Scott Ogden, Native Plant Specialist and Consultant
1111 W. Oltorf
Austin, TX 78704
Phone: (512) 448-0612

Texas Forest Service
Susan Sander, Staff Technician
P.O. Box 293127
Kerrville, TX 78029-3127
Phone: (830) 257-7744

Native Plant Demonstration Gardens

Before making your landscape plan, spend as much time as possible look-
ing at native plants in natural areas or established gardens.

Cibolo Nature Center
P.O. Box 9
Boerne, TX 78006
Phone: (830) 249-4616
Wildscape demonstration garden with trails through 85 acres of Hill Coun-
try native plants

Friedrich Wilderness Park
21395 Milsa Rd.,
San Antonio, TX 78256
Phone: (210) 698-1057
Trails through 150 acres of Hill Country native plants

National Wildflower Research Center
4801 La Crosse Avenue
Austin, TX 78739
Phone: (512) 292-4100
Fax: (512) 292-4627
Native plant demonstration gardens

Riverside Nature Center
150 Francisco Lemos Street
Kerrville, TX 78028
Phone: (830) 257-4837
Native tree arboretum

San Antonio Botanical Gardens
555 Funston Place
San Antonio, TX 78209
Phone: (210) 207-3250
Fax: (210) 820-3528
Native plant demonstration gardens

Natives of Texas
Spring Canyon Ranch
4256 Medina Hwy.
Kerrville, TX 78028
Phone: (830) 896-2169
Business Cell Phone: (830) 377-7683
Fax: (830) 257-3322
E-mail: bettyw@ktc.com
Web site: www.nativesoftexas.com
Native plant demonstration gardens

Zilker Botanical Gardens
2220 Barton Springs Road
Austin, TX 78767-8833
Phone: (512) 477-8672
Native plant demonstration gardens

Native Plant Nurseries

Be well informed! Most nurseries listed carry many species besides Hill
Country natives and will try to sell you what they have, native or exotic. If
you are interested in buying plants native to the Texas Hill Country, know
their Latin names and keep shopping until you find them.

Antique Rose Emporium
7561 E. Evans Road
San Antonio, TX 78266-2823
Phone: (210) 651-4565
Retail; associated with Brenham store

Barton Springs Nursery
3601 Bee Caves Road
Austin, TX 78746
Phone: (512) 328-6655
Fax: (512) 328-6517
Retail and wholesale; trees, shrubs, wildflowers, grasses, and succulents

Bastrop Gardens
Deena Spellman
316 Old 71
Cedar Creek, TX 78612
Phone: (512) 303-5672
Fax: (512) 303-5693
Web site: www.bastropgardens.com
Retail: take special orders, organic farm

Bloomers Garden Center
507 Hwy 95 North
Elgin, TX 78621
Phone: (512) 281-2020
E-mail: myoung@totalaccess.net
Web site: www.bloomersnursery.com
Retail; carries 50 percent Texas natives; good selection of agave and
succulents

Cibolo Nature Center
Mostly Native Plant Sale
P.O. Box 9
Boerne, TX 78006
Phone: (830) 249-4616
Annual sale in April; many experts available; call for exact date

Dodd's Family Tree Nursery
515 W. Main
Fredericksburg, TX 78624
Phone: (830) 997-9571

Fax: (830) 997-9216
Retail; trees, shrubs, grasses, wildflowers, and succulents

Fanick's Nursery
1025 Holmgreen Road
San Antonio, TX 78220
Phone: (210) 648-1303
Retail and wholesale; trees and shrubs

Gardener's Paradise
3600 Williams Drive
Georgetown, TX 78628
Phone: (512) 869-2985
Web site: www.georgetownnursery.com
Retail

Gardens
1818 W. 35th Street
Austin, TX 78703
Phone: (512) 451-5490
Fax: (512) 451-4523
Retail and wholesale; shrubs, grasses, wildflowers, and succulents

Gardenville of San Marcos
2212 Ranch Road 12
San Marcos, TX 78666
Phone: (512) 754-0060
Fax: (512) 395-8633
Web site: www.garden-ville.com
Wholesale and retail

Golden Eagle Landscape & Nursery
613 State Hwy. 27 East
Ingram, TX 78025
Phone: (830) 367-4144
Fax: (830) 367-2577

Web site: www.goldeneaglelandscape.com
Retail; trees and shrubs, plus custom ordering; specialize in large native
trees, 2-gallon native perennials, 5-gallon native shrubs, native grasses,
and good selection of cacti; landscape design and installation services;
Waterwise Design award winners in 2000; also do rainwater-harvesting
systems and irrigation

Gottlieb Garden
8263 Huber Road
Seguin, TX 78155
Phone: (830) 629-9876
Fax: (830) 629-9876
Wholesale; landscaping services; propagates Texas redbud, and a variety
of oaks

Green Cloud Nursery
Chuck Janzow
Boerne, TX 78006
Phone: (830) 249-3844
Wholesale; retail by appointment; native trees (including bigtooth maples)
and shrubs

Hill Country African Violets & Nursery
32005 IH 10 W
Boerne, TX 78006
Phone: (830) 249-2614
Retail; native trees (5-gallon and over) and shrubs

Hill Country Landscape Garden Center
P.O. Box 201297
13561 Pond Springs Road
Austin, TX 78729
Phone: (512) 258-1049
Fax: (512) 258-1527
Retail; trees, shrubs, wildflowers, grasses, and succulents

Kimas Tejas Nursery
962 Hwy. 71 E
Bastrop, TX 78602
Phone: (512) 303-4769
Fax: (512) 303-0816
E-mail: kimas@texasgrown.com
Web site: www.texasgrown.com
Retail

Landscape Market Place
1031 Austin Hwy.
San Antonio, TX 78209
Phone: (210) 822-1335
Fax: (210) 826-7152
Retail

McNeal Growers
Pat McNeal
P.O. Box 339
Manchaca, TX 78652
Phone: (512) 280-2233
Fax: (512) 291-0653
Web site: mcnealgrowers.com
Wholesale only; restoration, native and adapted grasses, ground covers,
and flowering perennials

Madrone Nursery
Dan Hosage
2318 Hilliard Road
San Marcos, TX 78666
Phone/Fax: (512) 535-3944
Web site: home.earthlink.net/~madronenursery/
E-mail: madronenursery@earthlink.net
Open by appointment only. Please phone ahead.
Container grows over 300 species of trees, shrubs, grasses, yuccas, vines,
and perennials with an emphasis on selections from the Edward's Plateau
and Trans-Pecos regions. Call for rare and hard-to-find species.

Medina Garden Nursery
13417 State Hwy. 16 N
Medina, TX 78055
Phone: (830) 589-2771
E-mail: medinagarden@wireweb.net or gardentx@yahoo.com
Retail; propagates many western Hill Country natives; have American
smoke tree, witch hazel, and madrones; two-acre demonstration garden

Milberger's Nursery
3920 N. Loop 1604 E
San Antonio, TX 78247
Phone: (210) 497-3760
Fax: (210) 497-3929
Retail; trees and shrubs

Native American Seed
P.O. Box 185 or
127 North 16th Street
Junction, TX 76849
Phone: (800) 728-4043
E-mail: info@seedsource.com
Web site: www.seedsource.com
Retail; seeds only

Native by Native Landscapes
602 W. Main
Johnson City, TX 78636
Phone: toll-free (866) 868-9933
E-mail: tess@moment.net
Web site: www.nativebynativelandscapes.com
Retail; native plant nursery and landscape design and installation services

Natives of Texas
Spring Canyon Ranch
4256 Medina Hwy
Kerrville, TX 78028

Phone: (830) 896-2169
Business Cell Phone: (830) 377-7683
Fax: (830) 257-3322
E-mail: bettyw@ktc.com
Web site: www.nativesoftexas.com
Retail and wholesale; native trees (including madrones), shrubs,
wildflowers, and grasses

Natural Gardener
John Dromgoole
8648 Old Bee Caves Road
Austin, TX 78735
Phone: (512) 288-6113
Fax: (512) 288-6114
Web site: www.naturalgardeneraustin.com
Retail

Nolan Creek Nursery
P.O. Box 287
798 W. Hwy 190
Nolanville, TX 76559
Phone: (254) 698-8622
Fax: (254) 698-8623
E-mail: nolancreeknursery@hot.rr.com
Retail; 90 percent natives

Olde Thyme Gardens
950 CR 365
Taylor, TX 76574
Phone: (512) 352-7673
E-mail: oldethyme@evl.net
Retail: 50 percent natives; trees and perennials; organic

Rainbow Gardens
8516 Bandera Road
San Antonio, TX 78250

Phone: (210) 680-2394
Fax: (210) 680-4505
Retail; trees and shrubs

Rainbow Gardens
12823 Nacogdoches Road
San Antonio, TX 78217
Phone: (210) 653-7655
Fax: (210) 657-7659
Retail; trees and shrubs

Rainbow Gardens
2585 Thousand Oaks
San Antonio, TX 78232
Phone: (210) 494-6131
Fax: (210) 494-9782
Retail; trees and shrubs

Schumacher's Hill Country Gardens
588 FM 1863
New Braunfels, TX 78132
Phone: (830) 620-5149
Fax: (830) 608-0914
Retail and wholesale; trees, shrubs, wildflowers, grasses, and succulents;
propagates many native plants; demonstration garden

Sweetbriar Nursery
Reid Lewis and Marie Kline
13999 FM 2305
Belton, TX 76513
Phone: (254) 780-4233
Fax: (254) 780-4234
Web site: www.vvm.com/~reid
Retail; seeds and propagates; 100 percent native; includes toothache trees,
wafer ash and Eve's necklace

Texzen Gardens
Glen Cooper
2008 W. Koenig Lane
Austin, TX 78756
Phone: (512) 454-6471
Retail

Where Wild Things Grow
Cindy and Dave Barrett
8915 Apache Trail
San Antonio, TX 78255
Phone and Fax: (210) 698-4372
E-mail: cbwherewild@aol.com
Deerproof landscape design and renovation (Leon Springs)

Natural Resources Conservation Service (NRCS)

The Natural Resources Conservation Service, formerly known as the Soil
Conservation Service, is an agency of the U.S. Department of Agriculture.
NRCS representatives help land owners with range management, flood
prevention, erosion control, water quality protection, and conservation of
streams and wetlands.

Bandera County
Kerrville Service Center
Joe Franklin, District Conservationist
Fred Reyna, Rangeland Management Specialist
420 Water St., Suite 101, Kerrville, TX 78028-5200
Phone: (830) 896-4911
Fax: (830) 896-3336
E-mail: joe.franklin@tx.usda.gov; fred.reyna@tx.usda.gov

Bexar County
San Antonio Service Center
Allen M. Collins, Soil Conservationist
Fernando Garza, District Conservationist
727 East Durango, Suite A-507, San Antonio, TX 78206-1204
Phone: (210) 472-5527
Fax: (210) 472-5525
E-mail: allen.collins@tx.usda.gov; fernando.garza@tx.usda.gov

Blanco County
Johnson City Service Center
C.A. Cowsert, District Conservationist
Main & Avenue G, Johnson City, TX 78636
Phone: (830) 868-7237
Fax: (830) 868-9296
E-mail: charles.cowsert@tx.usda.gov

Burnet County
Burnet Service Center
Richard Ellis, District Conservationist
101 N. Pierce St., Suite 2, Burnet, TX 78611-2527
Phone: (512) 756-4651
Fax: (512) 756-1921
E-mail: richard.ellis@tx.usda.gov

Comal County
New Braunfels Service Center
Kenda Thompson, Soil Conservationist
Bill Finch, District Conservationist
555 S. IH 35, Suite 220, New Braunfels, TX 78130-4879
Phone: (830) 625-5611
Fax: (830) 608-0573
E-mail: kenda.thompson@tx.usda.gov; bill.finch@tx.usda.gov

Gillespie County
Fredericksburg Service Center
Thomas Hammer, District Conservationist
1906 N. Llano St., Suite 107, Fredericksburg, TX 78624-2952
Phone: (830) 997-3349
Fax: (830) 990-4338
E-mail: thomas.hammer@tx.usda.gov

Hays County
San Marcos Service Center
Chris Perez, District Conservationist
501 Broadway St., San Marcos, TX 78666-7748
Phone: (512) 392-3202
Fax: (512) 392-5623
E-mail: chris.perez@tx.usda.gov

Kendall County
Boerne Service Center
Ted Bolzle, District Conservationist
39350 IH 10 W., Suite 8, Boerne, TX 78006-2522
Phone: (830) 249-2821
Fax: (830) 249-9120
E-mail: tbolzle@hotmail.com

Kerr County
Kerrville Service Center
Joe Franklin, District Conservationist
Fred Reyna, Range Management Specialist
420 Water St., Suite 101, Kerrville, TX 78028-5200
Phone: (830) 896-4911
Fax: (830) 896-3336
E-mail: joe.franklin@tx.usda.gov; fred.reyna@tx.usda.gov

Medina County
Hondo Service Center
Bruce Henderson, Soil Conservationist
Steven Riff, District Conservationist
257 State Highway 173 N, Hondo, TX 78861-6830
Phone: (830) 426-2521
Fax: (830) 426-2175
E-mail: bruce.henderson@tx.usda.gov; steven.riff@tx.usda.gov

Real County
Kerrville Service Center
Joe Franklin, District Conservationist
Fred Reyna, Range Management Specialist
420 Water St., Suite 101, Kerrville, TX 78028-5200
Phone: (830) 896-4911
Fax: (830) 896-3336
E-mail: joe.franklin@tx.usda.gov; fred.reyna@tx.usda.gov

Travis County
Austin Service Center
1106 Clayton Lane, Suite 210E, Austin, TX 78723-1080
Phone: (512) 459-1623
Fax: (512) 459-9073

Uvalde County
Uvalde Service Center
Bob Atkinson, Soil Conservationist
Rick Cantu, District Conservationist
103 Weeping Willow, Uvalde, TX 78801-6803
Phone: (830) 278-9197
Fax: (830) 278-3603
E-mail: bob.atkinson@tx.usda.gov; rick.cantu@tx.usda.gov

Texas Cooperative Extension Agents

Texas Cooperative Extension is a partnership between Texas A&M University, the counties of Texas, and the federal government. County extension agents and extension specialists provide research-based information on agriculture, environment, and natural resources as well as community and youth development.

Bandera County
Warren Thigpen/County Extension Agent-AG
2454 Hwy 16 North, Mansfield Park, Bandera, TX
Mailing address: P.O. Box 756, Bandera, TX 78003
Phone: (830) 796-7755
Fax: (830) 796-8121
E-mail: bandera-tx@tamu.edu

Bexar County
Jerry Warren, County Extension Agent-AG
Molly Keck, Extension Specialist-IPM (Fire Ant Program)
3355 Cherry Ridge, Suite 212, San Antonio, TX 78230
Phone: (210) 467-6575
Fax: (210) 930-1753
E-mail: j-warren@tamu.edu
Web site: http://bexar-tx.tamu.edu

Blanco County
Stephen Zoeller County Extension Agent-AG
200 N. Avenue G, Johnson City, TX
Mailing address: P.O. Box 189, Johnson City, TX 78636
Phone: (830) 868-7167
Fax: (830) 868-2348
E-mail: szoeller@tamu.edu
Web site: http://blanco-tx.tamu.edu

Burnet County
Wade Hibler, County Extension Agent-AG
1701 E. Polk St., Suite 12, Burnet, TX 78611
Phone: (512) 756-5463
Fax: (512) 715-5220
E-mail: wadehibler@tamu.edu
Web site: http://burnet-tx.tamu.edu

Comal County
325 Resource Dr., New Braunfels, TX 78132
Phone: (830) 620-3440
Fax: (830) 620-3446
E-mail: comal-tx@tamu.edu
Web site: http://comal-tx.tamu.edu

Gillespie County
William Botard, County Extension Agent-AG
95 Fredericksburg Rd., Fredericksburg, TX 78624
Phone: (830) 997-3452
Fax: (830) 997-6378
E-mail: w-botard@tamu.edu
Web site: http://gillespie-tx.tamu.edu

Hays County
Bryan Davis, County Extension Agent-AG
1253 Civic Center Loop, San Marcos, TX 78666
Phone: (512) 393-2120
Fax: (512) 393-2136
E-mail: by-davis@tamu.edu
Web site: http://hays-tx.tamu.edu

Kendall County
Jay Kingston, County Extension Agent-AG
210 East San Antonio St., Suite 9, Boerne, TX 78006
Phone: (830) 249-9343
Fax: (830) 249-2583

E-mail: j-kingston@tamu.edu
Web site: http://kendall-tx.tamu.edu

Kerr County
Roy Walston II, County Extension Agent-AG
3650 Hwy. 27, Kerrville, TX 78028
Phone: (830) 257-6568
Fax: (830) 257-6573
E-mail: r-walston@tamu.edu
Web site: http://kerr-tx.tamu.edu

Medina County
Wayne Scholtz, County Extension Agent-AG
1506 Avenue M, Hondo, TX 78861
Phone: (830) 741-6180
Fax: (830) 741-6182
E-mail: medina-tx@tamu.edu
Web site: http://medina-tx.tamu.edu

Real County
J. Mike McDougall, County Extension Agent-AG
Courthouse, Hwy. 83, Leakey, TX
Mailing address: P.O. Box 1050, Leakey, TX 78873-1050
Phone: (830) 232-6673
Fax: (830) 232-6040
E-mail: m-mcdougall@tamu.edu
Web site: http://real-tx.tamu.edu

Travis County
Jeff Ripley, Director
E-mail: j-ripley@tamu.edu
Robert Richter, Horticulture
Brad Pierce, County Extension Agent-AG
E-mail: bw-pierce@tamu.edu
Elizabeth Brown, Extension Agent-IPM (Fire Ant Program)

E-mail: ebrown@ag.tamu.edu
1600-B Smith Road, Austin, TX 78721-3541
Phone: (512) 854-9600
Fax: (512) 854-9611
Web site: http://travis-tx.tamu.edu

Uvalde County
Kenneth White, County Extension Agent-AG
3rd floor, Courthouse, Hwys. 90 & 83, Uvalde, TX 78802
Mailing address: P.O. Drawer 1708, Uvalde, TX 78802-1708
Phone: (830) 278-6661
Fax: (830) 278-2072
E-mail: kg-white@tamu.edu
Web site: http://uvalde-tx.tamu.edu

Texas Forest Service

The Texas Forest Service is dedicated to protecting and perpetuating both
rural and urban forests. Call a forester for the lastest scientific information
on forest insects, diseases, fire, ecology, and management. TFS is also a
source of government and private funding for tree and forest related proj-
ects.

Bexar and surrounding counties
Mark Peterson, Regional Forester
9350 S. Presa, San Antonio, TX 78223
Phone: (210) 633-1025
Fax: (210) 633-1005
E-mail: mpeterson@tfs.tamu.edu

Lon Patterson, Regional Fire Coordinator
6502 S. New Braunfels, San Antonio, TX 78223
Phone: (979) 220-0522
Fax: (210) 532-5101
E-mail: lpatterson@tfs.tamu.edu

Blanco County
Robert Edmonson, Staff Forester
P.O. Box 1718, Johnson City, TX 78636
Phone: (830) 868-7949
Fax: (830) 868-9040
E-mail: redmonson@tfs.tamu.edu

Gillespie and surrounding counties
Paul Hannemann, Chief Regional Fire Coordinator
David Hamrick, Regional Fire Coordinator
P.O. Box 1032, Fredericksburg, TX 78624
Phone: (830) 997-5426
Fax: (830) 997-3763
E-mail: phannemann@tfs.tamu.edu; dhamrick@tfs.tamu.edu

Hays and surrounding counties
Jan Fulkerson, Urban Wildland Interface Specialist
P.O. Box 1692, Wimberley, TX 78676
Phone: (512) 847-7387
Fax: (512) 847-7629
E-mail: jfulkerson@tfs.tamu.edu

Kerr County
Mark Duff, Staff Forester
Susan Sander, Staff Technician
P.O. Box 293127, Kerrville, TX 78029
Phone: (830) 257-7744
Fax: (830) 257-6444
E-mail: mduff@tfs.tamu.edu; tfskerr@ktc.com

Travis County
Clay Bales, Staff Forester
E-mail: cbales@tfs.tamu.edu
Eric Beckers, Staff Forester/Travis, Hays and Williamson Counties
E-mail: ebeckers@tfs.tamu.edu

Kim Camilli, Oak Wilt Coordinator/Statewide
E-mail: kcamilli@tfs.tamu.edu
Jim Carse, Staff Forester
E-mail: jcarse@tfs.tamu.edu
Jim Rooni, Regional Forester, Central Texas Region
E-mail: jrooni@tfs.tamu.edu
P.O. Box 15083, Austin, TX 78761-5083
Phone: (512) 451-2178
Fax: (512) 451-6946

Texas Parks and Wildlife Department

The Texas Parks and Wildlife experts listed here assist in the management
and conservation of natural resources. They develop active wildlife management plans, provide land owner incentives for managing rare species,
and can be called on to assist private land owners with technical guidance
on the management of game and non-game species.

Bandera County
Ray Aguirre, Wildlife Technician
310 Nicks Road, Comfort, TX 78013
Phone: (830) 995-5763
Fax: (830) 995-3872
E-mail: raguirre@hctc.net

Bexar County
Alan Cain, Wildlife Biologist
735 Trevino Rd., Pleasanton, TX 78064
Phone: (830) 569-6502
E-mail: atcain@awesomenet.net

Judit Green, Urban Biologist
Richard Heilbrun, Urban Biologist
134 Braniff, San Antonio, TX 78216
E-mail: juditg@aol.com; richard.heilbrun@tpwd.state.tx.us
Phone: (210) 348-6350

Blanco County
Max Traweek, Hill Country District Leader
309 Sidney Baker South, Kerrville, TX 78028
Phone: (830) 896-2500
E-mail: mtraweek@ktc.com

Burnet County
Trey Carpenter, Wildlife Biologist
213 Thomas Ridge Road, Burnet, TX 78611
Phone: (512) 756-2945
Fax: (512) 756-0815
E-mail: trey@tstar.net

Max Traweek, Hill Country District Leader
309 Sidney Baker South, Kerrville, TX 78028
Phone: (830) 896-2500
E-mail: mtraweek@ktc.com

Comal County
Rufus Stephens, Wildlife Biologist
P.O. Box 1802, Boerne, TX 78006
Phone: (830) 249-6887
E-mail: rufus@gvtc.com

Gillespie County
Max Traweek, Hill Country District Leader
309 Sidney Baker South, Kerrville, TX 78028
Phone: (830) 896-2500
E-mail: mtraweek@ktc.com

Hays County
Max Traweek, Hill Country District Leader
309 Sidney Baker South, Kerrville, TX 78028
Phone: (830) 896-2500
E-mail: mtraweek@ktc.com

Terry Turney, Wildlife Diversity Biologist
3331 RR 12 #102, San Marcos, TX 78666
Phone: (512) 396-0321
E-mail: terry.turney@tpwd.state.tx.us

Kendall County
Rufus Stephens, Wildlife Biologist
P.O. Box 1802, Boerne, TX 78006
Phone: (830) 249-6887
E-mail: rufus@gvtc.com

Kerr County
Ray Aguirre, Wildlife Technician
310 Nicks Road, Comfort, TX 78013
Phone: (830) 995-5763
Fax: (830) 995-3872
E-mail: raguirre@hctc.net
Max Traweek, Hill Country District Leader
309 Sidney Baker South, Kerrville, TX 78028
Phone: (830) 896-2500
E-mail: mtraweek@ktc.com

Medina County
Rick Taylor, Wildlife Biologist
P.O. Box 5207, Uvalde, TX 78802
Phone: (830) 278-9151 ext. 142
Fax: (830) 278-1570, attn: R. Taylor
E-mail: rltaylor@rionet.cc

Real County
Ray Aguirre, Wildlife Technician
310 Nicks Road, Comfort, TX 78013
Phone: (830) 995-5763
Fax: (830) 995-3872
E-mail: raguirre@hctc.net

Travis County
Trey Carpenter, Wildlife Biologist
213 Thomas Ridge Road, Burnet, TX 78611
Phone: (512) 756-2945
Fax: (512) 756-0815
E-mail: trey@tstar.net

Kelly Bender, Urban Biologist
146 El Camino River Rd., Bastrop, TX 78602
Phone: (512) 303-5943
E-mail: kelly.bender@tpwd.state.tx.us

Glossary

Alien Plant brought into an area by human activity

Alluvial Referring to soil deposited in valleys by streams

Alternate Referring to leaves set singly at nodes along a stem and alternating between opposite sides of the stem

Anther Male part of flower that produces the pollen

Asymmetrical Different on either side of a center line

Biodiversity Referring to the number of different plant and animal species

Bipinnate Referring to doubly pinnate compound leaves

Bottomland Flat, low-lying land on a river valley floor

Bract Small leaf on a small stem or beneath a flower, flower cluster, or branch

Browse Shoot, twigs, and leaves of woody plants eaten by wildlife or livestock

Bulb Underground plant part with buds surrounded by fleshy leaf bases

Buttressed Referring to a trunk with a base that widens toward the ground

Calcareous Referring to soil containing an excess of calcium carbonate

Caliche Deposit of calcium carbonate in soil of arid or semiarid climates

Capsule Dry, falling-away fruit that is formed from more than one flower

Catkin Slender, elongate flower cluster usually drooping, as on oaks, walnuts, and elms

Cedar brake Thick stand of cedar that is hard to move through

Check To crack or split while drying

Compound Divided into three or more parts, such as a leaf divided into leaflets

Constricted Pinched together

Deciduous Referring to a plant that drops leaves seasonally and remains leafless for part of the year

Elongate Lengthened

Endemic Living only in a small area

Epiphyte Plant growing on another plant for physical support only, taking no nutrients from the support plant

Exotic From another geographic area

Fallow Referring to land that was once plowed and is now unused

Fissure Crack in bark

Forb Broad-leaved plants, usually called wildflowers or weeds

Fungus Plant with no chlorophyll that lives on other organic matter, for example, mushrooms, mold, mildew

Generic Referring to the genus name

Hardwoods Trees, such as oak, cherry, and maple, that produce hard, compact wood

Herbaceous Does not become woody, usually dies back to ground each year

Hybridize To crossbreed different species

Infiltration Process of passing into or permeating the soil

Inflorescence Flower cluster

Infusion Liquid made by soaking a substance or part of a plant in water

Invasive Spreading into surroundings

Legume Family of plants with seed pods and with nitrogen-fixing bacteria on the roots

Limestone Sedimentary rock made mostly of calcium carbonate

Loam Crumbly soil made of mixed sand and silt with smaller amounts of clay

Lobe Rounded division of a leaf or petal

Margin Border or edge of a leaf

Mast Fruit, acorns, or other seed produced by woody plants

Mott Isolated group of trees, usually of the same species

Mulch Soil covering around plants that prevents water loss or erosion

Naturalized Referring to an exotic plant that has become self-perpetuating

Nitrogen fixation Process performed by microorganisms that removes nitrogen from the air and combines it with other elements so it can be used by plants

Node Joint of a stem, usually where a leaf is attached

Nodule Small knob or knot

Nutrient cycle Continuous sequence of changes for an element, such as nitrogen, that is an essential part of plant nutrition

Opposite Referring to leaves set in pairs at nodes along a stem

Palmate Hand-shaped, as leaflets radiating from a central point

Petiole Leaf stalk

Pinnate Referring to leaflets arranged opposite each other along the leaf stem

Pioneer plant One whose natural habitat is disturbed areas

Pith Spongy center in a stem

Prickle Sharp growth on bark of a twig

Recurved Bent backward

Reed Tall grass that grows in moist places

Riparian area Location at the edge of a stream, pond, or lake that is influenced by the water

Runoff Rainwater draining across the land in streams or sheets

Sepal Leaflike part at the base of a flower

Serrate Referring to a leaf margin with teeth that point forward

Simple Unbranched and single, such as an oak leaf

Slash Debris from fallen trees

Spore Reproductive body of a fungus or other lower plant

Stellate Referring to hairs that are star-shaped and branched

Sucker Shoot growing from the roots or lower stem of another plant

Tendril Slender plant part used for climbing

Terminal Tip end

Twining Referring to a vine that grows by wrapping its stem around a support

Understory Plants growing in the shade of larger trees

Vegetative Referring to the nonreproductive parts of a plant, such as stem, leaf, or root

Watershed Land area that drains into a particular stream

Whorl Ring of three or more leaves radiating from a central point

Windrow Line of branches left in a row, as if by the wind

Xeric Referring to dry conditions or ability to survive with little water

Xeriscape To landscape with plants that are well adapted to dry conditions

REFERENCES

Ajilvsgi, Geyata. *Butterfly Gardening for the South.* Dallas: Taylor Publishing, 1991.

Armstrong, W. E. *Managing Habitat for White-tailed Deer in the Hill Country Area of Texas.* Austin: Texas Parks and Wildlife Department, Wildlife Division, 1991.

Armstrong, W. E., D. E. Harmel, M. J. Anderegg, and M. S. Traweek. *Vegetation of the Kerr Wildlife Management Area and Its Preference by White-tailed Deer.* Austin: Texas Parks and Wildlife Department, Fisheries and Wildlife Division, 1991.

Correll, Donovan S., and Marshall C. Johnston. *Manual of the Vascular Plants of Texas.* Dallas: University of Texas at Dallas, 1979.

Cox, Paul, and Patty Leslie. *Texas Trees: A Friendly Guide.* San Antonio: Corona Publishing, 1988.

Diggs, Jr., George M., Barney L. Lipscomb, and Robert J. O'Kennon. *Shinners & Mahler's Illustrated Flora of North Central Texas.* Fort Worth: BRIT, 1999.

Enquist, Marshall. *Wildflowers of the Texas Hill Country.* Austin: Lone Star Botanical, 1989.

Erchsen-Brown, Charlotte. *Medicinal and Other Uses of North American Plants: A Historical Survey with Special Reference to the Eastern Indian Tribes.* Mineola, New York: Dover, 1989.

Everitt, James H., and D. Lynn Drawe. *Trees, Shrubs & Cacti of South Texas.* Lubbock: Texas Tech University Press, 1992.

Little, Elbert L. *National Audubon Society Field Guide to North American Trees, Eastern Region.* New York: Knopf, 1980.

Lynch, Daniel. *Native and Naturalized Woody Plants of Austin and the Hill Country.* Austin: St. Edward's University, 1981.

Nelle, Steve. *The Use and Management of Browse in the Edwards Plateau*.
Temple, Texas: United States Department of Agriculture, Natural Resources Conservation Service, 1994.

Nokes, Jill. *How to Grow Native Plants of Texas and the Southwest*. Austin:
University of Texas Press, 2001.

Schattenberg P. S. Cooper, J. Gallagher, and C. Adams. 2008. *Drought,
urban growth contribute to human-deer conflict in Texas*. Agnews.
http://agnews.tamu.edu/showstory. php?id=735.

Taylor, Richard B., Jimmy Rutledge, and Joe G. Herrera. *A Field Guide to
Common South Texas Shrubs*. Austin: Texas Parks and Wildlife Press,
1999.

Turner, B. L., Holly Nichols, Geoffrey Denny, and Oded Doron. *Atlas of the
Vascular Plants, Volume 1 and 2*. Fort Worth: BRIT, 2003.

U.S. Department of Agriculture. *The Use and Management of Browse in the
Edwards Plateau of Texas*. Temple, Tex.: USDA, Natural Resources Conservation Service, 1994.

Vines, Robert A. *Trees of Central Texas: A Field Guide*. Austin: University of
Texas Press, 1984.

———. *Trees, Shrubs, and Woody Vines of the Southwest: A Guide for the
States of Arkansas, Louisiana, New Mexico, Oklahoma and Texas*. Austin:
University of Texas Press, 1960.

Wasowski, Sally, with Andy Wasowski. *Native Texas Plants: Landscaping
Region by Region*. Houston: Gulf Publishing, 1991.

Winegar, Del. *The Explorers' Texas: The Lands and Waters*. Eakin Publica-
tions, 1984.

INDEX

Burnet County, 2

buckeye: Mexican. *See* Mexican buckeye; pale (yellow) (*Aesculus pavia* var. *flavescens*), 26, *134*, 210; red (*Aesculus pavia* var. *pavia*), 134; Texas (*Aesculus glabra* var. *arguta*), *133*, 210

buckthorn, Carolina (*Frangula caroliniana*), 5, 18, 23, 24, 82, *156*, 213

bluestem, King Ranch (Texas bluestem) (*Schizachyrium cirratum*), 37

buffalo gourd (stinking gourd, calabazilla) (*Cucurbita foetidissima*), *105*, 207

butterflies (by family or subfamily): admirals, 126, 130; red-spotted, 160, 164, 170, 171, 178; viceroy, 160, 164, 170, 171, 214. blues: azure, 104, 153; ceraunus, 120; marine, 113; Reakirt's, 112, 120; spring azure, 156, 164brushfoot: American snout, 179; (eastern) comma, 178, 180; goatweed, 208; mourning cloak, 145, 170, 171, 178, 180, 181; painted lady, 156, 164, 180, 184; question mark, 179, 180, 181; Theona checkerspot, 175; yellow-and-black zebra longwing, 149, 212. emperors, 179. fritillaries: gulf, 212; orange-and-black gulf, 149; variegated, 83, 101; 205. hairstreaks, 123, 126, 130, 136, 137, 167; banded, 160, 164; dusky-blue groundstreak, 79, 80, 81; Edwards,' 109; gray, 106, 109, 113, 156, 160, 191, 208; great purple, 186; Henry's elfin, 106, 114, 122, 173; Lacey's scrub-hairstreak, 108; olive, 69; soapberry, 172; white M, 178. metalmarks: fatal metalmark, 152. monarchs, 84, 85, 86, 184, 205. queens, 85, 205. skippers, 123, 126, 130, 167; Horace's duskywing, 209; silver-spotted, 113; yucca giant, 195, 196. soldiers, 85. sulphurs: lyside, 191; Mexican, 112; orange, 122; range, 12; southern dogface, 113, 116. swallow-tails, 167, 191, 214, 217; giant, 168, 169; spicebush, 138; (eastern) tiger, 138, 147, 160, 164, 168, 170, 171, 177; two-tailed tiger, 164, 168

butterfly food (nectar) plants, 88, 117, 139, 167, 173, 178

butterfly host plants: agarita, 14; buckeye, 173; buckthorn 156; cedar, 69; cenizo, 175; cherry, 164; cottonwood, 170; dogwood, 104; elm, 180, 181; guayacan, 191; hackberry, 179; hawthorn, 160; lantana, 184; linden, 178; milkweed 84, 85; mistletoe, 186; mountain laurel, 122; poison ivy, 80; possumhaw, 81; redbud, 114; redroot, 153; soapberry, 172; sumac, 79; swallow-wort, 83; sycamore, 177; tickle tongue, 169; wafer ash, 168; willow, 171; yucca, 195, 196, 197

bush palmetto. *See* palmetto, bush

buttonbush, common (*Cephalanthus occidentalis*), 5, 25, *167*, 214

Cabeza de Vaca, Álvar Núñez, 82

calabazilla. *See* buffalo gourd

canyon mock orange. *See* mock orange

Carolina basswood. *See* linden

Carolina buckthorn. *See* buckthorn, Carolina

Carolina snailseed. *See* snailseed, Carolina

catclaw:
Acacia greggii, 112
Acacia roemeriana (Roemer's acacia), *112,* 208
Acacia wrightii, 112

cedar. *See* juniper, ashe

cenizo (purple sage) (*Leucophyllum frutescens*), 26, 108, *175*, 215

Ceratocystis fagacearum. See oak wilt disease: cause of

chaste tree (*Vitex agnus-castus*), 62, 185

hummingbird food (nectar) plants, 10, 91, 125, 134, 139, 184, 206, 210, 211, 214, 216

insect(s): as disease carrier (oak wilt), 85, 59, 123; as food source, 10, 40; habitat of, 125, 176, 199, 205, 215, 218; insect tolerant plant, 125; insect vulnerable plant, 73; as plant pollinator, 92, 73
invasive plants, 37, 61–66, 69, 86, 95, 111, 120, 139; alien, 96, 110, 141, 200; exotic, 7, 67, 75, 90, 96, 110, 141, 148, 158, 165, 185, 200; naturalized, 15, 61, 62, 64, 73, 96, 143, 200
Italy, 197
ivy treebine. *See* cowitch vine

jaboncillo. *See* soapberry, western
Japanese privet. *See* wax leaf ligustrum
Jefferson, Thomas, 136
juniper, ashe (cedar, mountain cedar) (*Juniperus ashei*), 5, 13, 18, 24, 26, 69, 204; as cedar thickets, 5, 40; management, 30–43
jujube (*Ziziphus zizyphus*), 62, 158

Kendall County, 2, 19, 72, 74, 134, 135, 161
Kerr County, 2, 6, 74, 132, 133, 134, 161
Kerrville, Texas, 6, 71, 124
kidneywood, Texas (*Eysenhardtia texana*), 23, 24, 108, 116

Lacey, Howard, 124
landscaping and gardening: and conservation gardening, 21, 40; with native plants, 9–10, 12–16; and naturalized exotics, 61; for plant diversity, 17–18, 21–22, 40, 44, 60; with woody plants, 51, 53–60. *See also* deer, white-tailed: plants not favored by. For individual plant recommendations see plant chart, 204–218

lantana, Texas (*Lantana urticoides*), 26, 184, 216
Leakey, Texas, 72, 117
ligustrum. *See* wax leaf ligustrum
lime prickly ash. *See* tickle tongue
limestone, 3; Edwards, 3; Glen Rose, 3
linden (Carolina basswood) (*Tilia americana* var. *caroliniana*), 178, 145, 215
Lindheimer, Ferdinand, 193
Lindheimer's silktassel. *See* silktassel, Lindheimer's
Lipan Indians, 192
locust, black (*Robinia pseudoacacia*), 63, 64
Lomeria Grande. *See* Hill Country: Lomeria Grande
Lost Maples State Park, 72, 132
lotebush (*Ziziphux obtusifolia*), 158

madrone, 24, 38; Texas (*Arbutus xalapensis*), 13, 18, 23, 107, 207
maple: bigtooth (*Acer grandidetatum* var. *sinuosum*), 21, 23, 24, 72, 164, 132, 204; Uvalde bigtooth, 5, 72
mast, 24
medicinal plants: black willow, 171; bur oak, 125; chaste tree, 185; common elderberry, 98; evergreen sumac, 79; guayacan (soapbush), 191; huisache, 111; lantana, 184; linden, 178; little walnut, 137; pale buckeye, 134; pecan, 136; rusty blackhaw, 99; retama, 119; slippery elm, 181; Turk's cap, 139; Virginia creeper, 188; wafer ash, 168; white honeysuckle, 95
Medina River, 4
Medina County, 2
mescalbean. *See* mountain laurel: Texas
mesquite (honey mesquite) (*Prosopis glandulosa* var. *glandulosa*), 24, 26, 120, 158, 209
Mexican buckeye (*Ungnadia speciosa*), 82, 173, 215